THE STARTING SCHOOL SURVIVAL GUIDE

Sarah Ebner

THE STARTING SCHOOL SURVIVAL GUIDE

Everything you need to know when your child starts school

white LADDER

The Starting School Survival Guide: everything you need to know when your child starts school

This first edition published in 2011 by White Ladder Press, an imprint of Crimson Publishing, Westminster House, Kew Road, Richmond, Surrey TW9 2ND

British Library Cataloguing in Publication Data
A catalogue record for this book is available from the British Library

ISBN 978 1 90541 087 3

Typeset by IDSUK (Data Connection) Ltd
Printed and bound in the UK by Ashford Color Press, Gosport, Hants

14.9.'15

Per esser preparati al meglio a questa nuova avventura di "parents abroad"!

x

With love and thanks to my parents, Ann and Henry Ebner

Contents

Acknowledgements

Huge thanks must go, first of all, to my friend and ex-colleague Samantha Lyster, who came up with the idea for this book in the first place and persuaded me to put a proposal together. Thanks also to everyone at *The Times* for their help, especially all those who work with me online each day, and who have given me such support with my School Gate blog.

This book wouldn't have happened without Lizzy Kremer and Laura West at David Higham Associates or David Lester and Beth Bishop at Crimson Publishing, so many thanks to them too.

I would also like to express real gratitude to all my friends, those at the (real) school gate, the online one, and beyond. I couldn't have written this book without you.

And finally, I definitely couldn't have done this without the love and support of my family, particularly my parents, my husband, Brian, and the real-life experience of parenting two (gorgeous and wonderful) school-aged children, Jessica and Robbie.

Sarah Ebner, April 2011

Read my blog at www.thetimes.co.uk/schoolgate
And follow me on twitter @schoolgate

Introduction

Once you become a parent, advice is everywhere. And as you try to work out how to look after the small, helpless baby you somehow managed to create, you grab any advice on offer. But then, after a few years (and many sleepless nights) it stops.

"Where's the book?" one friend wailed to me when her son was nearing school age. She didn't know where to look for the best local school, nor how to apply. And when he got a place in Reception she had lots of questions – and no one to answer them.

In 2008 I set up an education blog for *The Times* called School Gate. The idea behind it was to "help parents through the maze of education". I soon realised that there were huge numbers of parents out there who wanted this guidance, as well as to talk about what their children were doing at school. School Gate fulfilled a real need.

That's why I wrote this book. It builds on what I've learnt from writing School Gate, as well as adding a lot more research and input from teachers, parents and education experts. Having two children of primary-school age also helped me along the way.

Over the last few years, countless people have asked me if there was a book about starting school which I could recommend. There wasn't. There were some which gave basic information, but I felt that parents needed much more than that. So, if you want to know how to find a good school, how to speak to teachers, how to deal with a clingy child, how to make friends (that's you *and* your child), how to organise playdates, what to do about headlice, and how to understand what on earth your children are learning, read on.

Starting school is a whole new world. This book will help you, not only to survive it, but to enjoy it too.

Author's note: I've referred to your child as male throughout, and teachers and authority figures as female. This is for consistency and ease of reading.

There are a number of comments from parents in the book. Some of them are taken from my blog and others from interviews done specifically for the book. This helps to explain why some have just a first name (even a pseudonym), while others give more details.

1

Choosing – and applying for – a school

Welcome to the next stage of your life! If you have a 3 or 4-year-old child (or, if you are impressively efficient, one even younger than that), you need to start thinking about applying for primary schools. Even though it can seem like a complicated and very, very confusing process, I'm here to help you to navigate your way through.

Choosing a primary school is probably one of the biggest decisions you've had to make as a parent so far. Schooling seems so important and grown up. It also seems like something that really will make a difference to your child's life. No one wants to get it wrong.

But life has changed since most of us simply pottered off to the nearest local school. Nowadays, choosing a school can be full of twists and turns.

So, now's the time to think about what kind of education you want for your child and to be honest about what kind of parent you are. Are you looking for small class sizes, lots of individual attention and good sport and music facilities? If so (and you can afford it), then you may want to consider private as well as state schools. However, if your priority is a local school (with local friends) within a short walk from your home, why look further than the school down the road? Providing you can get in, that is...

> “Choice? There isn't really a 'choice' of schools in London. You are just lucky if you get into the local primary which is near your home. We were three roads from our local primary and only got in on the second ballot. We were just lucky it was a great school.
> Juliette, mother of three children aged 10, 7 and 4”

In other words, problem number one is that the primary school which your child goes to is not totally your choice. You can list the schools you want and cross your fingers, or you can take the private route, but often it's the local authority or specific school which decides. However, there *are* ways to make the whole process more likely to work in your favour.

What's most important is not to wait for someone to tell you to apply. Admission to primary (and secondary) schools is not automatic. So, if you don't get moving, you might miss the boat completely.

Warning!

This is a very long chapter, covering choosing a school, applying, and appealing if you don't get a place. It's also not the most exciting (or amusing) chapter in the book (hey, applying for a school is a serious business), but needs must, and all this information is important. However, if your child already has a place at the school of your choice, many congratulations! You can skip straight to chapter 2!

Most local authorities (LAs) publish a leaflet or book about applying for schools. These may be advertised in your local doctor's surgery or library, or you could try your LA's website. Some LAs have particular staff dedicated to helping with the whole application process and/or offer a telephone helpline. You can also look up state schools in your area on the Government's Schools Finder website, http://schoolsfinder.direct.gov.uk, using your postcode.

The Government has recently set up a new search facility for schools called www.edubase.gov.uk. It allows you to search all educational establishments (including nurseries and independent schools).

WHEN DOES MY CHILD ACTUALLY START SCHOOL?

In England and Wales (Scotland and Northern Ireland are addressed on pp. 31–33), children don't have to start school until the term after they turn 5. In other words, your child is of "compulsory school age" on 1 January, 1 April or 1 September following their fifth birthday. However, they are allowed to start earlier than this - in the September after their fourth birthday - and most do. The school year runs from 1 September to 31 August, and children start their primary education in "Reception" (the dates are different in Scotland, and, as in Northern Ireland, the first year is called Primary One or P1).

The School Admissions Code sets all this out in detail, but is likely to be changed by the current Coalition Government. You can find out more about school admissions on the government website, www.education.gov.uk/schools/adminandfinance/schooladmissions

Some schools offer January start dates for children with birthdays which fall later in the academic year, although this is far less common than it once was. You should find out if your local authority runs this kind of staggered entry, as it may affect your decision about which school to send your child to.

The issue of so-called "summer babies", those born from June to August, is always a heated one, but a recent government review stated that children fell behind if they started school later than their peers. This is one of the reasons why the rules have been changed so that each child is legally allowed to start at 4.

From September 2011, primary schools *must* accept any child in the September following their fourth birthday. You are allowed to ask for this start-date to be deferred until later in the school year or until your child reaches compulsory school age, and you are also entitled to ask for your child to attend part time until he or she reaches compulsory school age. However, be aware that you do have to take up the place during the relevant academic year. If you decided to delay the entry of a summer-born child until he was 5, then he would miss out Reception completely and have to start in Year 1 (yes, this is crazy).

> "At the time, I thought that a January intake was a good idea as Danny seemed too young for full-time school when he was only 4 years and 5 months, and after only two terms of nursery. But in retrospect, I think an extra term of Reception would have been great especially as he loved his teacher. You could see the difference between the September and January intake kids by July; in particular, the January ones weren't as skilled with their writing."
>
> Joanna, mother of Danny, aged 5

You should similarly find out if you live in an area which has a middle-school system (such as Dorset or Somerset). This means they offer a first (or primary) school from the age of 5 to 8 or 9, then a middle school from 8 to 12 or 9 to 13, and then an upper (secondary) school after that. A three-tier system can make a real difference to your options at a later date. It's definitely worth speaking to other local parents to find out their views on this system and if they think it's better or worse than the two-tier system.

Should I think about Junior school now too?

Some schools have separate Infant and Juniors, on different sites and with different headteachers. This means that, when your child is in Year 2 (age 6 to 7), you will need to "apply" for a place in the Junior part of the school. However, your child's place will be assured – so don't worry about this for now!

I UNDERSTAND WHEN HE HAS TO START SCHOOL, BUT WHEN DO I NEED TO START PLANNING FOR IT?

Some say it's never too early to start stressing about school! If you are the kind of parent who plans well in advance, you may have moved into a particular area because you knew the local state schools were good, or put your child's name down for a very over-subscribed private school (from birth in some instances).

It's certainly true that if you are keen on a faith school, you will need to look into its admissions criteria. Getting in may involve regular visits to your local church, often for a number of years before applying. You should also check how near you need to live to that great state school down the road. This is the infamous "catchment" – the area around a school in which residents are assured a place. Sometimes the catchment area is all of a few hundred metres, which explains why certain houses cost so much. Schools also measure this in all sorts of ways – straight-line distance, shortest walking route or shortest route with street-lighting from the school, so it's worth finding this out. It can sometimes seem as if this is all just to confuse you.

You may well have heard scary stories about not getting into primary schools – especially if you live in an urban area. Recent reports have suggested that an increasing number of children don't get into their (well, their parents') top choice of school. Some even end up with no place at all. But before you start worrying, you need to choose which schools to actually apply to. True, you may not get into them all, but you may as well feel in control of the situation...

> "Just don't assume that your child will get into the school you want, even if you live nearby. It's not even assured if your child goes to the school's nursery – as we found out!"
>
> Janie

In an ideal world, we would all be able to choose the perfect school for our child – and he would get in. In reality, of course, this doesn't always happen, but it's still worth doing your research. That way you'll find out which schools you like, and which you don't.

WHAT ARE YOU LOOKING FOR?

When it comes to choosing a school, you need to think about what's most important to you. Are you looking for a school with after-school or breakfast clubs (a help to working parents) or one with a strong religious ethos? Do you want a small school (perhaps with just one class in each year) or are you happier with two or three forms? Are you interested in extra-curricular activities, such as sport or music? What kind of social mix are you hoping for? It's far better to find out about these things before your child starts at a school, rather than be disappointed later.

> "I think community is so important and makes a real difference. The larger a catchment area for a school, the more difficult it is to build a parental

community and feel part of something. That's why I went for a small local school with a tight catchment area. I also felt that it would be good for my children to walk to school each day rather than be squashed in the back of a car. ”

Susan, mother of three

The best thing to do is find out how your local schools fit your requirements. And then hope you get in.

MAKE SURE YOU VISIT

It's important to visit local schools and see what's on offer. Something which looks terrific on paper may not actually feel right to you in reality. What others call the "best" school may be too authoritarian for you (or your child), too big or too small. One way to visit is via a school Open Day. Either look on the school's website or ring up to find out when the next one is taking place. Whilst you're there, try to speak to the pupils themselves and also chat to the teachers. Get a feel for the place. Ask any questions you really want to know.

“ You have to decide what you are looking for. For some of my friends it was all about getting into the 'best' school, which meant the one with the highest results. But when I went to that school on a visit, I didn't like the atmosphere. Instead I went for a school which was thought of as 'good', but felt nurturing and had a lovely feel to it. ”

"Mumtotwo"

SPEAK TO PARENTS

If you can, you should also speak to other parents whose children attend the schools you are interested in (and their kids too). Contact the PTA (Parent Teacher Association) if you don't know anyone personally (ring the school and ask for details).

Ask around at places like your local toddler group, library or even doctor. People love to talk about education, but don't take everything that you hear as gospel.

It's right that you should listen to other people's opinions, especially those with children who are within a few years of yours. However, don't rely on rumours when it comes to assessing a school. Your child's education should be important enough for *you* to visit the school he might be going to for seven years.

Once you find out about the schools in your area, ring up and ask for a prospectus or take a look at a school's website. This should also give you an idea of its ethos, but don't be swayed by something too glossy. A school may be far better, or worse, than the way it sells itself.

What should you look for on a school visit?

Here are some things you should look for:

- are the children working?
- do the children seem happy? Watch for how they interact with each other and the staff.
- what are the displays of work like? Do they contain lots of spelling mistakes? Have they been up there for months? Are they all the same?

- what is your impression of the headteacher? How do the children behave around her? Does she seem friendly, but also seem to have authority?
- does the classroom seem welcoming?
- is the school clean?
- do the staff seem happy?
- how does the school encourage friendships? Is there a friendship bench in the playground, for example, or do they have a "buddy" system whereby older children befriend younger ones?
- if you can, sneak a visit to the toilets, these sometimes give you a very good idea of what a school is really like.

“Ask for a personal interview with the head. That gives you an opportunity to ask about things like policies on discipline and homework, clubs, and provision for special needs. It's also a way of finding out what's important to the head – do they encourage activities like music and drama, or are they only worried about SATs results? Can they offer extra help to children who are struggling, or provide more challenging work for gifted children?”

Kim Thomas, education expert

OFSTED REPORTS

If you're looking for information on local schools, you may want to look up recent Ofsted reports. Ofsted, the Office for Standards in Education, Children's Services and Skills, carries out regular inspections of schools and puts all its reports online. You can search for local schools under the inspections page at www.ofsted.gov.uk.

However, although Ofsted reports are helpful, and depressing if there is no chance of you getting into the nearest "outstanding" school, do check the dates carefully. If the last inspection was more than a couple of years ago, it may be horribly out of date. This applies to schools which received either a poor report or a great report (for example, a headteacher may have left, and the school may have gone down dramatically since).

Ofsted grades schools from 1 to 4. Grade 1 is outstanding; grade 2 is good; grade 3 is satisfactory; grade 4 is inadequate. When you're looking for a school, you really want it to be a 1 or 2. Be wary if it's a grade 4, and especially if it's in "special measures" as that usually means that there will be lots of changes to the staff, and parents may start removing their children. It is worth knowing that schools judged to be outstanding or good are only inspected once within a five-year period (those judged to be satisfactory are inspected every three years). Do read the report in detail; don't just look at the grades. It's always interesting to see which areas of the school (if any) rate as outstanding and which are poor.

When my children's school had an Ofsted inspection, I couldn't believe how accurate the inspectors were. They managed to sum up the school incredibly well after only two days.

Although the Ofsted inspectors can't tell you how you will feel about a school (you need a visit to do that) they can tell you an awful lot. They make judgements on the school's leadership, and its strengths and weaknesses. If they flag up any serious weaknesses, you should take this on board. You should also take notice if the inspectors mention a problem with bullying or discipline. This is something you could raise on a school visit or a chat with the headteacher.

Each time they do a report, Ofsted inspectors also write a letter to the pupils who attend the school. It's definitely worth reading this, as it's usually a good summary of what they have found.

Note: Wales, Scotland and Northern Ireland all have Ofsted equivalents. You can find out more at www.estyn.gov.uk (Wales), www.hmie.gov.uk (Scotland), and www.etini.gov.uk (Northern Ireland).

LEAGUE TABLES

You can check league tables via the Government's own website, www.education.gov.uk/performancetables.

These tables show how well children do in their National Curriculum tests (commonly known as SATs) aged 7 and 11. If you are particularly concerned about how your child will be pushed at school, check how many children, aged 11, achieve a level 5 in their tests. This at least shows that the more able children are being stretched, and that it's not just about getting the children through with a level 4 (the level the Government thinks they should reach).

But league tables are not the be-all and end-all. They have a number of flaws (counting absent children as having failed, for example) and I would take more notice of the Ofsted reports and word of mouth. League tables very often reflect the school's intake, and many schools prepare their children for SATS by cramming in the final year.

“We went for atmosphere and scale over academic performance, thinking that at this age, if the child is happy, that is half the battle. A more intimate environment seemed right for our child, as did it being a faith school – though we had some misgivings about that (lack of variety, not the real world, rather privileged cohort). But religious input if not overdone can be very nurturing, reassuring and in our child's case, familiar. ”

Leonie, mother of Kate, aged 7

“ My words of wisdom are:

1) Visit the school and find an excuse to slip off (i.e. go to the loo). Then take a peek through classroom windows and feel the vibe of the school.
2) Don't follow what your friends are doing and choose a school so your child will be with their mates or you with yours. Choose what is best for your child.
3) Don't get too hung up on Ofsted and league tables. My priority was 'will my child be happy?' not 'will my child be pushed enough?'
4) Talk to other parents and work out the general demographic of the school.
5) Do a dummy run of the walk/drive in rush-hour traffic.

It is so important that they are happy at primary school. It sets them up for the rest of their learning. Come secondary school I'll worry more. ”

Barbara, mother of three children aged 8, 7 and 4

WHAT KINDS OF SCHOOLS ARE THERE?

There are various types of state school, all of which receive funding from local authorities. They follow the National Curriculum and are regularly inspected by Ofsted. State schools are sometimes known as "maintained" schools (because they are maintained or financed by the local authority).

Community schools

A community school is run by the local authority, which not only employs the staff and owns the land and buildings, but also decides on the "admissions criteria". Most local schools will be community schools.

Foundation and Trust schools

Foundation schools are run by their own governing body (see p. 142 for more on governors) which employs the staff and sets its own admissions criteria. The governing body (or perhaps a charitable foundation) usually owns the lands too. There aren't many of these kinds of schools in the UK (only around 2%).

Faith schools

England's education system traditionally developed in partnership with the Church. This partly explains why there are so many faith schools in the country - although there has also been a huge rush to set up more in recent years. Faith schools make up around a third of all state schools in England (around 14% in Scotland).

There are two types of faith schools in the state sector (see p. 14). Most are Church of England or Catholic, but there are also Moslem, Hindu, Sikh and Jewish state schools. All have to follow the National Curriculum, be inspected by Ofsted and comply with the statutory admissions code.

Voluntary-controlled schools

These are run by the local authority. In other words, like community schools, the local authority employs the school's staff and sets the admissions criteria. However, school land and buildings are normally owned by a charity (mainly religious) which appoints some of the members of the governing body. These type of faith schools tend to be easier to get into, as they don't necessarily give priority to children with a particular religious background.

Voluntary-aided schools

These are run in a similar way to the foundation schools, with a governing body which both employs the staff and sets the admissions criteria. They have more independence than voluntary-controlled schools as they set their own admissions criteria. However, the criteria must be in accordance with the Schools Standard and Framework Act 1998, Education and Inspections Act 2006, and Statutory School Admissions Code. Not all voluntary-aided schools are faith schools.

Faith schools are seen by many as an escape from the state system, particularly for those who can't afford private education. However, they also tend to arouse very strong opinions. Sometimes this comes down to a straight split between those who are pro or anti religion. But it's not always that obvious. Some people don't want their taxes paying for children to go to a school which their own kids wouldn't be allowed to attend. Others don't like these schools because they feel that they work against community cohesion, and that taking the Catholic, Moslem, Hindu, Sikh and Jewish children away from each other leads to a less tolerant society.

The admissions criteria for faith schools usually give priority to members of a particular faith (often demonstrated by regular attendance at church, for example) and when you apply, you will often need to fill in a "supplementary information form" (or SIF) which may detail how often you have been to church/mosque/synagogue or, for example, whether your child has been baptised. You may also need a reference from the leader of your place of worship.

For many popular schools you may have to think very far ahead – and show that you have been a committed member of a congregation for several years before you apply for a place. However, that is still no guarantee your child will get in.

Many good faith schools are also very over-subscribed. Because so many parents apply for places for their children, they will often invoke a geographical rule (how near you live to the school) as well.

Many families with young children have "found" religion in recent years, leading to accusations of hypocrisy. You need to decide for yourself whether a religious ethos is a must for you, or, if you are not religious, whether you want your child to be taught in a school with a religious bent.

> "I have a problem with faith schools, even though my children go to one! To me as an atheist, having the existence of God presented to them as fact is a problem. However, I've realised that it's something I have to live with and that I made the choice of school with my eyes wide open."
>
> Gary

> "I know some people seem to hate faith schools, but if they are such a bad thing why do so many people want to go to them? My local Catholic school offers a better standard of education than a community school and I am very happy with it. I feel that I am entitled to choose the best education for my child."
>
> Simone, mother of three girls

Free schools

This is the newest type of state school and a flagship policy for the Government. Free schools are set up and run by parents, teacher groups or other organisations (including charities). The Education Secretary, Michael Gove, announced the first tranche in 2010, and they're a varied bunch, many with a faith background. They include two Jewish schools in London, a Hindu school in Leicester, a Sikh school in Birmingham and three with a Christian ethos. Only 40 have been approved so far, but there are more to come. The first free schools will open in September 2011.

Most of the free schools have an ethos which will set them apart from normal state schools. They will not have to follow the National Curriculum and can also boast smaller class sizes.

You still apply for free schools through the local authority. However, in their first year you may have to apply for some directly, because they'll be too late for the local authority process.

Academies

Primary schools are now allowed to become academies - which, like free schools, means they are state-funded but independent of the local authority. There is a strong drive to encourage more of these, and they also have more freedom over what they teach and don't have to follow the National Curriculum. However, like free schools, you apply for them via the local authority.

Community and foundation special schools

Special schools cater for children with specific special educational needs. These may include physical disabilities or learning difficulties.

There are far fewer special schools than there used to be. This is because, in recent years, the political will has been towards "inclusion" and educating all children in mainstream schools, but with extra help provided. So, even if your child has a statement of special educational needs (known as a co-ordinated support plan in Scotland), he will usually be educated in a mainstream school. That's not to say that a special school is an impossibility, but trying to get a place at one will almost certainly be a real battle. If you want your child to have a shot at getting in, it's really important to start the process as early as possible.

> "This is such a huge issue and parents really need to be forceful about it. It's cheaper for education authorities to provide one-to-one help in a mainstream school than it is to send the child to a special school, and it often seems as if this financial reason is why decisions are made. Parents are told that they need to 'try mainstream first'. This is false. There's no reason why a child should be unhappy in a mainstream school for a few years when he needs a special school."
>
> Kerry, mother of three

In a special school, the staff to child ratio will be smaller, there will be better facilities and also more access to specialist input. It may seem like a no-brainer that this is the place which will bring out the best for your child. But this, I'm afraid, could signal the beginning of a fight to get your child in.

When it comes to catering for children with learning difficulties such as dyslexia, some of the best schools are in the private sector, and although it is sometimes possible to get financial help from your local authority to cover some of the costs of a school like this, it won't be easy.

> “My advice for any other parent who is choosing a school for a child with special needs would be to go with your instincts. You know your child better than anyone. Schools, Educational Psychologists and Local Authorities like to think they do, but they invariably don't.
>
> Katrina, mother of two boys, both with special needs”

What if I'm not sure whether my child has special needs?

Many children don't actually get diagnosed with special needs until they are in school and it can then be a real struggle to find the right schooling for them. We look at this more in chapter 11. However, if you already have concerns about special needs, go to your GP or speak to your health visitor to get the ball rolling. You can then ask the local authority to carry out an assessment of your child's needs (called a Statutory Assessment). You should ensure that you submit as much professional evidence as possible for this, for example by using an independent educational psychologist.

The authority is obliged to let you know within a certain period of time (currently six weeks) if they intend to carry out the assessment, and it is this assessment which determines whether they think your child needs a statement. If a statement is agreed, it becomes legally binding and sets out the support which your child will need in school.

If your child has a statement of special needs, then, legally, you have a right to say which state school you want them to go to, either mainstream or special. However, that right doesn't necessarily mean a smooth journey. Your pre-school may be able to help you, but make sure you are fully aware of any form-filling they do on your behalf. You need to make sure they have all the information they could need.

> My son is autistic and we have had wonderful support from his pre-school SEN (special educational needs) person who is managing his transition from nursery into school. The statementing process was not as difficult as I envisaged but it is so drawn out! He was just diagnosed a year ago and the process takes a ridiculous 26 weeks. Luckily I had already selected a (mainstream) school and got him a place there. If we'd been relying on the statement for that we'd be in a real pickle. The school is very supportive and had a teaching assistant in place for him before he started.
>
> Liz

The SEN Code of Practice (http://tinyurl.com/654j79u), should be regularly consulted. Unfortunately, many mainstream schools don't bother to follow its principles unless pulled up. You have the right of appeal at every stage of this process and you should make sure you use it. Local authorities often back down just before an appeal hearing.

Educating a child with SEN always brings extra challenges. If you are not looking for a special school, you need to be particularly careful to find out how a mainstream school would help your child.

Make sure you identify what might really affect him (for example, will he thrive in a smaller school?) and ask specific questions when you visit. If your child needs help while at school, find out what is on offer. Try to speak to the school's special needs co-ordinator (known as the SENCO) to get an impression of how the school can help your child. If your child has special needs, you will be dealing with the SENCO on a regular basis so it's important you get on with her.

> “Word of mouth is very important. Ask how many children there already are in the school with your child's issue or disorder. If there are lots, then it is probably a good school. Do not rely on Ofsted reports as an outstanding Ofsted school may not be at all interested in special needs. Go to support groups and ask where people who have children with a similar disorder are educating them.”
>
> Kerry, mother of three

It might be that you don't actually find out about the school you need, or how it would help your child, until he is a little older. You are then able to apply for it at a later date.

Two very useful parent-support organisations to contact are the Independent Parental Special Education Service or IPSEA (www.ipsea.org.uk) and SOS-SEN, The Free Independent Helpline for Special Educational Needs (www.sossen.org.uk).

Note: the new Government is also looking at SEN provision in schools and changes will soon be on their way.

Private schools

You may decide that you want to send your child to a private - or fee-paying - school. These have their own vocabulary, starting with “pre-prep” schools, which run from ages 2 to 7 (many prep schools also have pre-prep sections).

Generally speaking, private or “independent” (from government control!) schools offer very good facilities and smaller class sizes than state schools. They also tend to have more socially exclusive intakes. Some are very academic, and will ask your child to take a test before they will accept them. They may also want to meet you and your child, although I wouldn't worry too much about this.

What they are looking for is a child who is sociable, aware and interested. Not every private school tests its younger pupils when it comes to applications, so it's always a good idea to ask the school directly.

Private schools set their own admissions requirements, which vary from school to school. After the Early Years Foundation Stage (which includes Reception) they don't have to follow the National Curriculum. Nor do their pupils have to take National Curriculum tests (Sats). It's definitely worth a visit to see what kind of educational experience they would offer your child.

Private schools are funded by fees and charitable bequests. Naturally, money is a key consideration, and with many private schools, you are paying anything upwards of £6,000 a year per child (which is on the low side). When you sign up, you will often find that you are agreeing to a more expensive school life - the uniform will cost more than its state school equivalent, and so will school trips and the many extra-curricular activities.

If you're interested in a private school for your child, you should take a look at the Independent Schools Council website, which has a helpful Parents Zone section, www.isc.co.uk/ParentZone_Welcome.htm

If you send your child to a private school, you will probably find that they have more homework (yep, even aged 4 or 5) than they would get in a state school. You will have to decide if that's right for your family. If it's the extra-curricular activities which appeal, remember that there is always the alternative option of sending your child to a local (i.e. free) state school and paying for after-school music or sport instead.

Every independent school must be registered with the Department for Education and they are regularly monitored by either Ofsted or the Independent Schools Inspectorate (www.isi.net).

Not all private schools are high flying, and neither are all children. You should do proper research to make sure you choose a school which is right for your own child. Private schools often work for children with special needs, or those who really seem to need a smaller class (so they don't get "lost"). Private schools also differ remarkably – for example, there are many which are single-sex. If you have an idea of which private secondary school you would like your child to go to, you should check to see if the private primary is a "feeder" for that school. In other words, find out if children from a particular primary school get priority for the secondary.

"I chose a private school because I have a particularly bright child and I wanted her needs to be met. I feel that state schools are better at catering for the under-achievers than the over-achievers. It was really about the smaller class sizes and her getting more individual attention. This is exactly what she is experiencing."

Vanessa, mother of two, aged 4 and 1

"I always thought I would send my sons to the local state schools, but, when it came to it, I realised that we weren't guaranteed entry into our brilliant, but very oversubscribed local state school. When we looked at the other schools in the area, the private ones were really appealing, particularly because they had great after-school clubs and brilliant facilities."

Vivienne, mother of two boys

Some state primary schools "feed" into secondary schools. This means that most of the children will go to a particular secondary school, although it's not necessarily automatic. You should find out if your primary school does have priority or a connection with a particular school when it comes to secondary school allocations. This is common with some faith schools.

APPLICATION CRITERIA

The number of schools you can apply for will vary depending on your local authority. It's fine to apply for very popular schools which you may not get into (there's always hope!) but don't do this with all three of your choices. Otherwise your local authority will offer your child a place anywhere - and you may not be happy with their choice.

Although you put the schools you want in order, the schools themselves don't see this, so don't worry that you won't get a place at a particular school because you put them second or third. The aim is for you to get your favoured school. So, if your child was fortunate enough to get a place at all your choices (apparently it does happen, but I imagine it's rare), then he would be offered a place at your top choice. The other preferences are there in case the top choice is full (the more usual scenario).

You will usually have to send your application forms off by mid-January the academic year before your child will attend, at the latest.

There are various government publications to help you with your choice of school, and how to apply. One of the most obvious starting points is the *Primary and Secondary Schools, Admissions and Appeals* document, which you can download from the internet at http://bit.ly/govtguidetoapplying. There is also more information on applying for a school place on the Directgov website (www.direct.gov.uk/en/Parents/Schoolslearninganddevelopment/ChoosingASchool).

ADMISSIONS CRITERIA

Applying for schools really is complicated. But one thing is absolutely vital: you must follow the admissions criteria. And if you don't meet the criteria – either geographically, for example, or on a faith basis – then you need to have a plan B.

The criteria might change every year, so always check. Don't rely on what happened in the past to tell you what will happen in the future.

Many schools have too many applicants for each place. Reception classes in English and Welsh state schools have a maximum of 30 pupils (fewer in Scotland, and Northern Ireland), so places are often allocated according to their admissions criteria. To make sure everything's managed fairly, schools and local authorities must follow strict rules which are set out in the School Admissions Code and the School Admission Appeals Code. These don't apply to private schools.

You can actually see the admissions criteria and the number of applicants for school places the previous year in the *Information for Parents* booklet provided by your local authority. Sometimes this can be quite shocking – 150 applicants for 30 places at your chosen school, for example.

The Government's admissions code makes it clear that so-called "looked after" children (those in care) should be given top priority. After this, the criteria will vary slightly, but will usually include some of the following:

- Special needs. If your child has special needs, definitely mention this. Don't hold back. Schools must cater for children with special needs and often prioritise them.
- A disability. This refers to a child or a parent who may have a disability which would make it hard to travel to a school far away.
- Siblings of children already at the school (so you're usually alright if you've already got one child in). Note that it's only if your child has siblings *still* at the school. If your other children have already left, this is no help at all.
- Geographical location. Don't be shy about phoning the school you are interested in and asking how they work out the

catchment area. Be aware that it can actually change from year to year.

- Faith school criteria. This usually involves attendance at a local church, mosque or synagogue.

Having a child in a school's nursery is no guarantee of a place in Reception (although it may in a faith school). You will still have to fill in a school application form if your child is in the nursery.

HOW TO APPLY

Filling in the forms

Once you've made your choice, you need to make sure you fill in the forms correctly. You would be surprised how many parents don't do this.

Your local authority co-ordinates applications for state primary schools. If you're applying to two schools in separate authorities, you only complete one application form for the authority where you live, regardless of the location of the schools.

However, don't think that's all you need to do. Some schools (particularly faith schools) will also require you to fill in a "supplementary" form which you then return directly to the school. Read through these extremely carefully. And if you do require some kind of statement or reference from your religious leader, or your GP, don't leave it to the last minute to get it. Plan ahead.

Possibly the most important lesson when it comes to primary (and secondary) school admissions is to do whatever the school wants. So if you're not sure about this, telephone the school, and ask.

Don't lie

Getting into the right school is a very stressful and touchy issue for many parents. We have all heard stories of those who rent a house near a good school to get in, and yes, this can work (I know some of these parents myself). However, you do have to live in the house in question (not just use its address), and local authorities are trying very hard to crack down on those who abuse the system.

Never give a false address on an application form as the information you give may be checked. It has been suggested that parents who do this should be prosecuted – or at the least, that their children should lose their places.

> "Lying to get your child into a school they wouldn't otherwise have got into is criminal behaviour. It just shows how self-centred you are, and how little you care about the rest of society. Remember, if you lie, you are stopping another child, who should have got in, from getting into a school. What kind of lesson are you teaching your child?
> Jackie, mother of three, aged 9, 7 and 4"

I'VE APPLIED: WHAT NOW?

I'm afraid that the next thing you have to do is wait. You will probably have sent off your application form by January, but offers don't usually go out until March or April. Most local authorities send out letters and put the information online.

WHAT IF YOU DON'T GET IN?

> "I felt utter despair when we were told that our daughter hadn't got a place at any of the three schools we put down. I didn't know such a thing could happen and I felt I had let my child down. Other people tried to be nice, but I felt patronised because they were so sympathetic. It was awful."
>
> Julia, mother of two, aged 6 and 4

Local authorities have a legal duty to offer your child a school place, but not to offer a place at a particular school. If you then choose to turn down the place you have been offered for your child, that's your preference.

So, there's always the possibility of bad news when it comes to school admissions. And it can be incredibly hard if your child doesn't get into the school you set your heart on. But is there anything you can do about it? This might seem as if it's the end of the road, but it isn't. You do have options...

Put your child's name down on a waiting list

Ring up the school you wanted - and any others which you liked - and put your child's name on the waiting list. There can be a lot of movement on waiting lists so it is definitely worth putting your child's name down. A school administrator should be able to tell you where you are on the list. If the school you have been offered was not your first (or second) preference, some local authorities will automatically put your name down on the waiting list for these higher ranked schools.

Waiting lists operate under the same criteria as admissions. In other words, if geographical location was an important factor when it came to getting a place, this will still determine where you are placed on the list.

I would definitely recommend staying on a waiting list – and you are allowed to stay on for as long as you'd like to – but it's good to have another option too. If you just rely on moving up a list, you need strong nerves. A friend of mine got her son into a very good local school this way, although she didn't find out until the July before he started.

You can accept an offer at one school and stay on the waiting list at another one. Or accept an offer at both a private and state school while you are making up your mind (however, if you have paid a deposit for the private school and then decide not to send your child there, you will probably forfeit the money).

Because your child doesn't actually have to start school until the term after he turns 5, you could decide to keep him at nursery and hope that a place will become available at some point. However, there are no guarantees that it will!

Don't dismiss the school you have been offered

If you've been offered a place at a school you don't want, don't dismiss it out of hand. Instead go and take another look at it. You may find that, after a visit, you have a different view. Sometimes a school's reputation does not reflect the reality.

Visit alternative schools in your area

It's certainly worth looking at other schools near you, and these should include those with and without places. Even though the offers have gone out, you could make an application to any of these schools and, if they are full, you can still ask to be put on their waiting list.

Unfortunately, local authorities are not always particularly helpful, so make sure you ask them to send you the list of schools with places, or ring schools directly. Legally, as you now know, LAs don't have to provide a place until after your child turns 5. This could be some months away for your son or daughter, and, because of this, it can sometimes seem as if they are in no rush to assist you.

Make an appeal

If you had your heart set on a particular school, you can appeal to try to get in. However, be realistic about this – it's extremely hard to get into a primary school on appeal (mainly because infant class sizes are legally restricted to 30 children unless there are "exceptional" circumstances).

Appeals for school places have grown hugely in the last decade (the most recent figures showed that there were almost four appeals for every hundred pupils) and they aren't usually successful. In fact, while the number of appeals has risen, the number of *successful* appeals has fallen.

In other words, don't depend on an appeal. If you're honest with yourself, you will know if you have a good case. If you simply wanted your child to go to this school, but didn't get in because of the admissions criteria, then you have little chance of being successful.

If you do decide that you want to appeal you should send back the form included in the letter you received from the local authority. If an appeal form is not included, you should send your own letter, stating that you wish to appeal.

You must send in your form or your letter as quickly as possible. Appeals usually take place just a few weeks after places are offered.

You do not need to write out your whole case immediately, just say why you want to appeal and give as many reasons as you can. The focus must be on why it is this school and *only this school* that your child must go to.

Your appeal should contain as much evidence for your case as possible. Make sure this is clear and easy for the appeal panel to understand. Above all, you need to refute the school's arguments for not accepting your child.

Grounds for appeal may include:

- social/medical needs which you feel can only be addressed in this particular school.
- a mistake by the local authority (for example, you feel that you should have got a place on a geographical basis and that the distance from the school to your house has been wrongly measured).
- unfair application of admissions criteria (for example, your favoured school asked for a monetary contribution, which is not legal unless on a voluntary basis).

You are allowed to appeal for one particular school even if you have been offered a place elsewhere.

The appeal will take place in front of an independent panel of three to five people.

Further advice and information on admissions and appeals can be found from the Advisory Centre for Education (ACE) at www.ace-ed.org.uk. I also suggest reading Ben Rooney's book, *How To Win Your School Appeal* (A & C Black Ltd, 2009).

Whatever happens, keep up a brave face

Try not to let your child see how upset you are if he doesn't get into your first choice of school.

If your appeal fails, he will have to go to the school on offer (unless you have a very good Plan B such as a private school or new house) and will need to make the best of it. Children are very adaptable, and it really is best not to start them off on the wrong foot. You don't want them to feel they are going to a second-rate school.

> "We were very disappointed when we didn't get into the school we wanted, but I would say to other parents that it is worth trying out the school you're given and to be positive about it. You never know, it might exceed your expectations."
> Julia, mother of two, aged 6 and 4

Below is a very quick summary about applying to schools in the rest of the United Kingdom

Scotland

If you are a Scottish parent, the situation is slightly different and, happily for you, less complicated.

In Scotland, local councils divide areas into catchments, and children in one catchment usually go the same local school (although denominational schools may have wider catchments).

However, parents do have the right to choose a different school for their children. This is done by making a "placing request" for the school you want your child to attend. By law, the council has a "duty" to grant this request wherever possible, but you may not get a place if there are too many applicants for the places available. The local authority can also hold back places for children who might move into the catchment area at a later date.

Your council will usually contact you regarding school places in the December, January or February before your child is supposed to start. However, if you don't hear from them, be proactive and get in touch. If you want your child to go to a school run by another council (perhaps you live on the boundary) you must, of course, contact that council too.

The Scottish school year is also different from that in England. Children (usually aged between 4½ and 5½) start primary school in August, rather than September. All those born between the March of one year and the February of the following year are placed in the same year group. However, it is possible to start your child at school early – if the council agrees that this is good for your child.

Find out more at the Scottish Schools Online website, which has details of every Scottish school, www.scottishschoolsonline.gov.uk.

For information on private education contact the Scottish Council for Independent Schools (SCIS) via their website, www.scis.org.uk.

The council must let you know about schools for the following August by the end of April. You usually need to apply by mid-March at the latest.

Northern Ireland

All children between the ages of 4 and 16 are entitled to a free school place in Northern Ireland. Children normally start primary school aged 4.

- The law actually states that where a child reaches the age of 4 between 1 September of that year and 1 July of the following year, that child should begin compulsory education the following September. So, if a child's fourth birthday was on 30 March 2011, he would start compulsory education in September 2011.
- But where a child turns 4 between 2 July of that year and 31 August of the same year, that child won't begin compulsory education until September of the following year. For example, if a child turned 4 on 5 July 2011, he wouldn't start compulsory education until September 2012.

The main types of schools receive funding from their local Education and Library Board (which is where you get the relevant application form), or directly from the Department of Education. Your Library Board can give you a list of all the schools in your area and, as in England, you will be asked for a list of your preferred schools.

You can take a look at the inspection reports of the country's schools at www.etini.gov.uk/index/inspection-reports and find out more at www.nidirect.gov.uk.

Wales

Wales operates a similar system to England although it has its own School Admissions Code.

As is the case in England, you have the right to express a preference for your child's school, but if a school is oversubscribed, it may give preference to pupils in its own "catchment area".

One difference between English and Welsh applications is that in Wales, local authorities don't have to run co-ordinated admission schemes. In practice, many do so.

And finally...

Above all, remember that *you* are vitally important when it comes to your child's education. If you talk to your children (and listen to them talk back to you), read them books, take them to the library and museums, and show a general interest, they will thrive. Teachers and schools are important but so are parents. How your child develops is not just up to the school they go to. You are an incredibly strong influence on your child's education, whichever school he gets into.

2

Preparing your child for school

Congratulations! The hardest part – finding a place for your child at school – is over. Now you can take a deep breath, relax. . .and start preparing for the day when your child puts on his uniform and enters a whole new world.

I'm not one for pre-school Mandarin classes, nor for kindergarten Kumon, but if you want to know if you can help make the transition to school a little easier, the answer is yes.

> "The experience of starting school undoubtedly creates a stress response in children. What was surprising to us was that cortisol levels – which are associated with stress – rose around two to four months before starting school. There could be a number of reasons for this but it does suggest that stress levels in anticipation of starting school begin to rise much earlier than we anticipated."
>
> Dr Julie M Turner-Cobb, Senior Lecturer in Health Psychology at Bath University

Clearly, we should try our hardest to make sure that our children aren't stressed before they turn up at the school gate. This doesn't mean hot-housing them to within an inch of their lives. Instead it means giving them the confidence to start their school lives happy, and ready.

SEVEN SENSIBLE – AND PRACTICAL – SUGGESTIONS TO MAKE THE TRANSITION EASIER

1) Talk about school!

Explain where it is, take a visit if possible (if you can't go inside to see the classroom, look from the outside) and strip away any fears your child may have. Listen to your child's questions and answer them as honestly as you can. However, being positive will be more helpful than giving off a negative vibe, even if you hated school yourself. Basically, big up "big school"!

> "My mum didn't actually tell me that I was starting school. I know it sounds ridiculous, but she dropped me off one day and I had fun. The next day she dropped me off again and I wasn't happy. I still remember trying to escape!
> When we had Laura, I made sure that we kept her aware of what was going on."
> Gary, father of a daughter aged 5

2) Practise social skills

Your child may soon be one of 30 in a class. This means that he needs to learn how to mix with others.

Mixing well and socialising is often easier if your little darling has attended a nursery or regular playgroup, but you may still need to encourage listening to others - not just talking over them - sharing and taking turns.

Using role play can help if you have any concerns about this. Use your child's brothers and sisters, teddies, dolls or puppets and set up school scenes. Get one teddy to say goodbye to his parent after drop-off; get another to ask if he can join in a game or activity. You could even seat everyone together at a practice lunch.

If you can persuade your child to tidy up after an activity, the teachers at school will be thrilled and little Emily or Oscar will immediately earn some precious Brownie points.

These social skills are crucially important from both your child's and their teacher's point of view. Having them makes that cross over to "big school" much, much easier and means that your child is far better prepared for learning.

3) Give them some independence and responsibility

It's true that teaching your child to be independent can be hard on both of you, on an emotional and practical level. As a parent, "letting go" can be a struggle as you realise that your child relies on you less. And on a practical level, allowing your child to do things himself nearly always means it takes longer.

Gaining independence takes practice, so, in the few months before school starts, encourage your child to go to the toilet by himself, wash his hands (with soap) and dry them. I can't over-stress the importance of this - it is a real nightmare for teachers if a child starts school and isn't properly toilet trained, and it's embarrassing for a child as well. Although your child might still have the occasional accident, it's far better for everyone if that's very much the exception rather than the rule.

Leave time for your child to start dressing himself in the morning, even if it's just pulling on socks and pants, and help him to put his shoes on (this will come in very useful for games lessons). It's also a boon if he can hang up his own coat as they can easily get kicked around and disappear when they fall off children's pegs.

Your child should have an idea of how to blow his nose (not always that easy; my 5-year-old is still no pro) and know that he should cover his mouth when he coughs or sneezes. If you can help your child to learn how to use a tissue properly, go to the top of the class!

Do not confuse giving your child independence with letting him do what he likes! That is not a lesson for happy parent/child relations.

4) Make friends: for you and your child

If you know other children who are going to be in your child's class, arrange some playdates or get-togethers in the park. The school may have a list that they can send around, or the PTA (Parent Teacher Association – you're going to need to learn this new vocabulary, and there's more on them in chapter 7) may organise some events too. Don't be scared to get in touch; you'll also find it easier if you recognise a friendly face at the school gate.

5) Get into a school-type routine

Some people swear by this – moving into a routine some months before school starts, so that rushing out of the door, uniform on, by 8.20am, isn't a shock when the time finally comes. I'm not so sure, as I think you should cherish any opportunity not to worry about the school run before you have to. However, I would recommend encouraging your child to eat a proper breakfast (cereal, toast, or a hot dish such as eggs or porridge if you have time, plus a drink) because they need the energy to get through the day. They may also not have eaten since about 6pm the previous evening. If you can, do encourage them to speed up a little though. Otherwise the rushing-to-school-shock, when it comes, might be too great.

6) Tough sweet love

Cut down on the day-time snacks. Once at school, your child will have set times for eating. It will help hugely if he gets used to this, and not endless grazing on demand, before he starts. It would also be beneficial if he got used to eating fruit (which local councils supply to state schools for infants) and drinking water, instead of squash, fizzy drinks or juice. Milk and water tend to be the only drinks on offer in most schools.

7) Eat together

Once your child starts school, he will find himself eating snacks and lunch with lots of other children. If he has spent the previous four years eating alone - while you hover in the background creating culinary delights - he may find this difficult, not to mention noisy.

You can help by eating meals with your child and by inviting friends and family around to eat too. It may sound like a minor issue, but some children find this transition one of the hardest of all, and simply stop eating properly while at school.

It's extremely useful if your child can use cutlery properly – in other words, knives and forks, as well as spoons! Try to encourage this as much as possible, as it not only encourages good eating habits, but also works on fine motor skills (which will help in other areas such as with his pencil grip – more on this on p. 170).

CLOTHES MAKETH THE CHILD. . .

Many schools still ask children to wear school uniform. Don't buy this too early as your child will grow, leaving you with a whole load of brand new clothes which no longer fit. However, don't leave buying uniform until the week before school starts - the shops will be completely chaotic and you will be left in shock. I did this once, and will never do so again.

Barnardo's and Citizens Advice recently published a poll showing that 73% of parents with children of school age find the whole business of school uniform, bags, shoes and other items incredibly stressful. There is government guidance on the fair pricing on uniforms, but many schools ignore it, leaving some parents with real financial worries. After all, do children really need a PE kit which costs £15 because it has a logo on it and is bought from a specific supplier?

Make sure you check if the school allows you to buy unlabelled uniform from any supplier, as supermarkets are often much cheaper. It's also a good tip to find out if your school has any second-hand sales (many run stalls at the summer fête).

> Our school lets Reception and Year 1 children wear jogging bottoms, which is great for the ease of getting on and off by both parent and child. Rather than spend £9.99 per pair in the uniform shop, I could buy them for £4 at Asda with perfectly acceptable quality and durability. The difference in cost with my two sons is £36 each year, which is quite shocking.
>
> Caroline G, mother of two sons aged 7 and 4

Make life easier through choosing the right clothes!

Your child will enjoy school more if he feels happy and confident. Although you won't be there, you can help this in so many ways, even via the clothes he wears. So, keep it simple.

Do. . .

- Buy jogging bottoms or skirts with elasticated waists – these are so much easier to put on and take off.

- Buy shoes with Velcro on rather than straps or more complicated fasteners (such as laces).
- Buy coats which are easy to do up – toggles may be simpler than zips or buttons.
- Buy the uniform together, letting your child get involved, choosing the colour of the shirt, for example, or type of socks (this should mean he'll be keener to wear them).
- Help your child to learn how to fold his clothes and keep them together in a neat pile – it will help to guard against them getting lost.

Don't. . .

Buy tights unless you're convinced that your 4 or 5-year-old is perfectly capable of taking them off to go to the toilet – and then putting them back on again.

If your child is starting at a school which doesn't have a uniform, be warned, this can be expensive too. Buy hard-wearing clothes, but prepare yourself for peer-group pressure to wear more fashionable outfits as your child gets older.

Label everything!*

This won't stop your hunt for missing sweatshirts, but at least it gives you a chance of finding them again. Show your child where the label is, so he knows how to check if it's his or not.

* Labels are essential, even though it really is a pain to put them on everything. It's so easy to lose things and can cause real stress between children and parents ("What, you've come home without your sweatshirt *again*?"), and parents and the school. Teachers don't take very kindly to being accosted by parents complaining about lost sweatshirts, and then admitting that they didn't put a name on them ("it's blue with the school logo on it" doesn't really help). At least if you've named items, you have some hope of finding them!

There are various labelling options, from sew-ons and iron-ons, to stickers. Some mums just write the name on, and that works too, as long as you use a permanent marker pen.

Buy a name tag in a particular colour (so your child can recognise it, even if he or she can't read).

LITTLE EINSTEINS: HOW MUCH DOES MY CHILD NEED TO KNOW ACADEMICALLY BEFORE HE STARTS SCHOOL?

Personally I don't think it helps a child to be pushed too much at an early age. In fact, if your son or daughter is going to be attending a state school, it may not be that beneficial for them if they are already very adept at reading and writing when they start. It actually risks them getting bored (sad but true). However that's not to say you shouldn't encourage pre-schoolers to explore and develop before they start school.

> "It doesn't matter if a child comes in not knowing anything. They all have different starting points and we move on from where they are at. I have always been happy to suggest to parents ways in which they can make learning at home fun and parents can prepare their children by playing games and talking to them about starting school. It shouldn't be about sitting down and getting them to write lines of letters."
>
> Ruth Vered, Reception class teacher

School has changed since you went there, and in the Early Years, children learn in a play-based rather than formal learning environment (there'll be more about this in chapter 8). If your child has been to nursery, the curriculum will be a continuation of what they did there. They won't be sitting behind individual desks learning their ABC by rote.

Seven sensible ways to help learning

1) Talk, talk and talk some more

Don't let your child sit in front of the television or computer the whole time. Instead ask questions and initiate conversation. Pre-schoolers are fantastic fun to talk to and have brilliant imaginations.

All this talking will also help when they start school as they may be more open to your enquiries about what they have done all day (although don't be too disappointed if they just say "nothing").

2) Read books together

Point out letters if you think your child is ready (many are), but stick to lower case, not capitals (this is how they will be learning their letters in school). It's often useful to start with the letters in your child's name and then add a few more onto that as time goes on. Try to encourage recognition of – and help them write, if they can – their own name. Alphabet fridge magnets are great for this; so is writing their name on any pictures they may draw.

Show your child which way words are read (from left to right), talk about the pictures in the books you read together, and ask questions about them too (what happened etc). Point out words elsewhere too, for example, on shops and road signs.

If your child is keen to read, then help him to do so, but be warned that most children are now taught to read phonetically (see pp. 165–168 for more on this). This means they need to know the sounds of the letters rather than their names (the letter "c" makes the sound "c", as in "cat", rather than "cee" as in "sea").

3) Encourage dexterity

Fine motor skills are responsible for the body's small muscle groups. They are used in tasks such as sewing, playing musical instruments and (vitally for small children), drawing and writing.

Your child needs to develop strength in his fingers and control when writing. Although this will come with time (many young children soon get over any problems simply with age, as their muscles get stronger), you can help too.

Buy/borrow (large size) beads and play with them. Also use playdough and clay (all that finger work is very useful) and thread laces too. Encourage your child to paint, draw, use scissors, trace, colour in and do dot-to-dots.

4) Encourage writing: if your child is ready

You can encourage writing, but don't be too disheartened if your child (especially if he's a boy) finds this hard. Holding the pencil correctly is very important, but some children are simply not physically ready for this at age 3 or 4. Don't worry too much about this as it will come eventually! What you can do instead is work on their fine motor skills and show them the right way to hold a pencil so at least they have this in their mind.

You can also do "writing" in other ways. Try swirling your finger in sand, for example, or using a paint brush. Some children love drawing pictures for stories and dictating the words, so creating their own book.

5) Help develop concentration

There are so many ways to do this, from putting together a jigsaw puzzle, creating something out of old junk (loo roll tubes come in very handy) or simply playing a board game (Orchard Toys have some excellent examples. My favourites include Shopping List and Tummyache).

6) Be creative

You've probably been doing this already, but all that cooking, cutting, sticking and painting is excellent, not just for fine motor skills, but also for developing creativity and enhancing a child's imagination. It's also a lovely way to spend time with your child (as long as you're not averse to mess).

7) Think of a number!

Writing and reading aren't the only things your child will learn to do at school. Maths is the other main focus of attention. Help them get a head start here by following a few useful (and fun) tips.

- Compare things and match them: are they the same, different, bigger or smaller?
- Get them to help you to put socks together, play odd one out and see what your child picks up on.
- Measure things - show your child the scales when you cook for example, and count things, from building blocks or stairs, to the number of red cars you see parked on your street.
- Sing number rhymes (anything from *Ten Green Bottles* to *One Potato, Two Potato*).

As the time for starting school gets ever nearer, keep talking about it (but not so much that you drive your child mad), and encourage any elder siblings or cousins/friends to join in too (but tell them to leave out any horrible stories!).

Suggested books to read together

Topsy and Tim Start School, Jean and Gareth Adamson (Ladybird, 2009)
This book has a great tone. Topsy and Tim are a little bit worried about going into Reception, but they're not too scared. However, they do notice that school is bigger and noisier than nursery.

I Am Too Absolutely Small For School, Lauren Child (Orchard, 2007)

This book is so imaginative and beautiful; your child should love it. It's the story of how big brother Charlie tries to persuade his feisty little sister Lola how important it is that she should go to school and start learning. "What if 11 eager elephants wanted a treat, how would you count up how many treats that would be?" he asks at one point. Lola isn't sure, but by the end, she's had fun and made a new friend too. Excellent.

Silly School, by Marie-Louise Fitzpatrick (Frances Lincoln Children's Books, 2007)
This is the perfect book for the start of the school year. It tells the story of Beth, who simply doesn't want to go to school, despite her family's best efforts at persuasion. Clever and very nicely illustrated, it ends with a happy Beth who doesn't want to leave the classroom!

Kevin Goes to School, by Liesbet Slegers (Clavis Publishing, 2009)
This is a delightful book, which is written very simply – so hopefully your child may soon be able to try and read it with you. It tells the story of Kevin's first day, what he does and how he soon makes friends, despite being a little shy.

Harry and the Dinosaurs go to School, by Ian Whybrow and Adrian Reynolds (Puffin, 2007)
Harry (and his dinosaurs) start "big school" and make friends with Jack. Harry fans will like this, as it's gentle and fun.

Starting School, by Janet Ahlberg and Allan Ahlberg (Puffin, 1990)
This is a lovely story, which follows children through their first term at school and gives lots of detail about what goes on. It comes highly recommended by children, their parents and teachers.

THINKING AHEAD: TIPS FOR WORKING PARENTS

The school day is not brilliant for those of us who work. But if at all possible, do try to drop off and pick up your child on their first day.

You should be sent the dates long in advance, and it will certainly help your child to settle in. Try to find out if parents are expected to stay at school with their children for any length of time. Many schools discourage this, as children are usually fine once their parents are gone! However, some invite you in for a half hour or so, and it's always good to be prepared (your child will probably pick up on your stress if you're worrying about an early-morning meeting you're suddenly late for). You don't want to feel that you need to rush.

If you are starting a job once your child starts school and will be altering your childcare arrangements, try not to make too many changes all at the same time. If it's possible, introduce new people well before your child starts school or, alternatively, wait a few weeks until they are settling nicely.

There's more on schools, working parents and the difficulties of finding childcare in chapter 7.

PARENTAL WOES

Now we've discussed what should help your little one start school, let's move onto another vital area – you. Starting school isn't just hard for your child, it can be very hard on you too.

It doesn't matter whether it's your first child, second, only or last, you're sure to have some kind of reaction when they're grown up enough to go to school. It's good to know that you are not alone.

Know that you are allowed to feel sad in the run-up to school and that this may be months beforehand (it is all quite normal). I felt very melancholy when my son started his last term at nursery, and when I wrote about it on my blog, was pleased to find that many felt the same way (though others were quite dismissive, generally in a rather superior way).

“My ‘baby’, my daughter, starts school in September and I feel a bit sad. It’s frightening how fast the time goes, like sand slipping through your fingers. It’s wonderful to see them grow and thrive (my daughter is almost frighteningly brave, independent and assured and will love school) but for many of us it’s bittersweet.

Leah, mother of a stepdaughter aged 18,
a son aged 8 and a daughter aged 4”

With the preparations complete, you should be ready for the next stage: the big day itself.

3

The first day approaches

The previous chapter should have helped you in the run-up to the first day of school. But what about the practicalities of the first day? How does it all work? And how will your child react? In this chapter, I'll take you through the practical and emotional aspects of the big first day.

As the big day approaches, be prepared and don't panic. How's that for earth-shattering advice? Obviously this may prove easier for some of us than others. But however you feel inside, the most important thing is to *appear* calm. Children pick up on their parents' moods extremely easily.

HOME VISITS OR IN-SCHOOL MEETINGS?

All schools like to appear welcoming to parents, but they carry this out in different ways. Most will have a meeting, usually at the end of the summer term before your child starts. This could be when you find out what class your child is in, for example. However, some schools leave this meeting until the very beginning of the autumn term, just a few weeks before your child's first day.

A number of schools also offer home visits before a child starts, and these can be very good at introducing children (and parents!) to their teachers. It's usually a Reception class teacher who goes on the visit, but be aware that schools may not have finalised classes by the time of the home visit. This means that your child could be visited by the other class teacher (yes, this is odd!).

Some parents worry about home visits, as they think they will involve teachers "prying" into their lives outside school, or judging them. However, the visits are actually set up to help the child: he gets to feel special and meet his teacher, while the teacher gets to see him in his own environment. Yes, this does mean they get an idea of how you live, but it's for your child's benefit. For example, a teacher can gauge whether there are lots of siblings in the house or even if a child is likely to have had a proper breakfast before he starts the school day.

> "It's all about adding pieces to the jigsaw. And it helps you to see what the child is going to need. After all, that's the priority."
>
> Julia Skinner, ex-headteacher of a primary school in Bristol

> "The teacher and teaching assistant came round to our house for about 15 minutes a few weeks before my son started school. It wasn't a long visit, but he loved it, possibly because they brought round a big box of Lego! I thought it was a great opportunity to ask any question we wanted to without loads of other parents being there and thinking we were talking rubbish!"
>
> Mark, father of a daughter aged 6 and a son aged 4

Not all schools run school visits. If they don't, they will usually offer some other way for a child to meet the teacher before starting school formally. Some schools even invite children in for a morning or afternoon a week during the summer term. If you are desperate to take your child to look round the school before the beginning of term and haven't been offered either of these options, give the school office a ring to ask if you can come another day.

Wherever the meeting takes place, it will follow a familiar format. The teacher, usually accompanied by a teaching assistant, will introduce herself to the child and ask about his friends or what he likes doing (let's hope he doesn't spill the beans on his penchant for beating up his little brother). They may ask your child to draw a picture (so that there will be something familiar on the wall when he starts school) and they will usually take a photo of him to put by his peg when he arrives. They may also speak to you about any issues you may want to raise – which is when the teaching assistant could helpfully start distracting your child.

Whatever the set-up, you should see the pre-school meeting as an opportunity to help smooth the transition of your child from home or nursery to school. This is your chance to point out any concerns – for example, that your child may be shy, not comfortable in groups of children, or anxious about eating with lots of other children in a school canteen. Give the teachers any tips on how to put your child at ease.

> " Always take schools up on the offer of visits before your child starts. If they don't do visits, ask why not! On the visit make sure you find the playground, the lunch hall, and where the toilets are. Take photos of the journey to school, playground and classroom with a digital camera. Print the photos out and make a little book with your child to talk about before they start. "
>
> Rosie, Early Years teacher

Many schools also have Reception information packs which they give to parents, either by hand at a pre-school meeting, or by post. These should include useful information about the workings of the school day (although they might just contain lovely, but rather useless pictures of happy, smiling children).

TEACHING TIMETABLE

It's highly unlikely that your child will start school and launch into full days straightaway (although a number of private schools do this). So, it's vital that you know what the school timetable will be for the first few weeks. The school will send you this information and you may find that your school has short days for the entire first term - which can be very trying for parents juggling younger children or jobs.

Many schools stick to the usual start times for new children, but have different finishing times. Sometimes this can mean dropping your child off at 8.45am and picking them up again at 11am! Whatever happens, make sure you're not the mum or dad who's blissfully unaware of all this - and whose mobile then rings to inform them, just when they're beginning a yoga class or in a vital work meeting...

> "The staggered settling in worked well for my children because it was so gentle and took it at their pace. It started with two hours on the first two days and then four hours for the rest of the week. It worked for them, but it all relied on a parent being at home or available. You definitely need to make arrangements in advance."
>
> Jill, mother of three children, aged 7, 4 and 2

Generally speaking you won't get a choice about the school starting dates, but they are commonly later than the usual beginning of the academic year, which means that you can take a later, and cheaper, summer holiday.

Schools settle in children in different ways, but nearly always in small groups. Some settle the older children in the year first, or those with older siblings. But while this may suit parents the most (you can wave goodbye to all of your school-aged children earlier and get your life back), I can't say that I agree. Such a policy means that younger children (who aren't used to the school) join a class which is already busy.

> "I thought the school settling in process was very unhelpful. My daughters didn't know anyone else, missed the first few weeks of term while other children formed friendships, and had to join a class that was very busy. I also worried that it meant experienced parents would form an even tighter clique.
> Kate, mother of twin daughters born at the end of June"

I have no idea why so many schools settle their children in this way, but completely sympathise with parents who have told me that it's the wrong way round! Surely the younger children, or the ones not familiar with the school from dropping off and picking up older siblings, should have the most gentle introduction. I have one friend whose school recently implemented this policy and she was delighted. Her daughter, born in July, knew nobody who was starting Reception with her. She began with four other children, and it was a huge success.

However, many people won't have this positive experience and it's something which you should think about raising, either before you start school or once you are there. True, this may be too late for your own child, but it could help others – and we all care about the greater good, don't we?

Schools usually settle children in over a few weeks (generally between two and four weeks for the whole class).

Interestingly, Kate, who's quoted above, joined with some other parents to take this issue up with the school governors. The Reception class teachers at her school are now looking into changing how they settle in new children for the future.

HOW WILL YOUR CHILD REACT?

Starting school will have a different impact on different children. For example, when my son started school, he was excited, but not at all nervous. This may well have been due to his personality (laid-back and sunny), but I'm guessing that it also had a lot to do with the fact that he was used to going to school because his older sister had already been there for three years. It didn't hold any fears for him.

However, it's not uncommon for children to be anxious about starting school and you can help by being low key and talking about school as a normal part of life. Share books about school, talk about it, and be encouraging without going over the top. Help your child to see school as simply the next stage of the nursery they enjoyed so much.

> “ My son was so thrilled about starting school he asked me to take him along to his old nursery after his first day to show off his smart new uniform – officially a 'big boy' at last! Obviously, parents can

do a HUGE amount to make a child think that going to school is exciting and fun.
Helena

"Starting a new school can be an anxious time for children and parents, quite understandably. New teachers feel anxious too! However, for young children and their parents it can be particularly difficult. You can never tell which child is likely to find the transition difficult: sometimes it can be one who has seemed very confident and outgoing before, so don't be surprised or unduly shaken if there are teething troubles."
Gillian Low, Head of the Lady Eleanor Holles School, Hampton, Middlesex

TALK ABOUT IT

You should, by now, have worked out that I truly recommend communicating with your child about starting school! So, I hope that you'll have talked to him about this next stage in his life and given him an idea of what to expect on the first day.

- Whatever the settling-in arrangements, give your child an idea of what's going to happen, where he is going to go and how long they will be there.
- Ask him if he has any questions for you and let him know that the school day will include some of his favourite things (you can find this out from a teacher in advance) such as painting or doing jigsaws.
- Make sure you tell him that you – or his carer – will be there at the end of the day.

- Whatever you do, don't dismiss your child's worries or make him feel stupid for having them.
- Answer his questions as best you can, or ring up friends with older children and ask them. That way your child can see that you are trying to help.
- Explain that he should speak to the teacher or teaching assistant if there are any problems.

Some people (that's children *and* their parents) find that the constant talk of "starting big school" can become tiresome. Although you do need to prepare your child for school, you may find that it's wise to "back off" a little in the final few weeks before it actually starts.

> "Don't over-do the emphasis on school. If you go on and on about it for weeks, your child can get really worried about it. We did that with our daughter and it back-fired! It's fine to mention school, but be matter-of-fact about it. You also want to enjoy the time you have with your child before they have to go off to school. Don't waste it all by only talking about the next step in their lives!"
>
> Leila

Some parents didn't enjoy school, but you need to be careful not to pass your feelings (er, prejudices) onto your children. It's *their* experience that's relevant, not yours. Things have changed a lot since you were at school (as you will see). So start off with a constructive frame of mind.

Have a plan of action for yourself to take your mind off it all. Meet other mothers for a coffee, go to the gym, take your younger child on a playdate or go straight to work. Just don't give yourself lots of time alone to mull over events!

Don't forget to. . .

- Have school clothes laid out the night before – it'll save any last minute panics.
- Make sure the camera is charged the night before for that all important first day at school photo.
- Leave early (you might want to set the alarm a little earlier).
- Take some tissues (for you, not your child!).

> "There is nothing worse than stressing over being late on the first day of school because the anxiety crosses over to the child. We did a dummy run of our journey to school a couple of mornings beforehand to see how the traffic was."
>
> Viki, mother of two sons aged 5 and 2

THE FIRST DAY ARRIVES: AT LAST

The first day of starting primary school really does symbolise a new stage of your child's development - and can be overwhelming for both of you. Some children find the ranks of parental photographers too much to handle. Other parents find that the simple truth of their child growing up gets too much for them.

> "On the first day, I made sure we were really well prepared. I decided to get there an hour early and we went for a walk. I wanted to give Lila some one

on one time with me, and it worked brilliantly. When we got to the school gate, we were both in a relaxed, happy mood. ”

Tamar, mother of two daughters aged 4 and 2

LEAVING YOUR CHILD ON THE FIRST DAY

When it comes to classroom etiquette, schools have different rules. Some like to get rid of parents as quickly as possible, while others let them stay for a short while at the beginning (one school I came across allowed parents to stay for the first half an hour for the entire Reception year). Don't worry too much about this on the first day – just do what feels right for you and your child. Usually this does involve coming into the classroom, hanging up coats and bags and then having a kiss and cuddle goodbye.

Don't hang around for longer than you need to, just because *you* are feeling a bit melancholy. It's probably better for your child if you go sooner rather than later.

Take the lead from him, and if he seems happy, it's time for you to go. Don't draw out the goodbyes. Teachers find that it's disruptive to have parents in the classroom for too long.

“ Quite often I think the worry is more about the parents than the children. They know their child is now entering full-time education and that they'll probably be there for the next 16 years. It's stressful for them. ”

Tanja Perez-Williams, Reception class teacher

Some youngsters will cling on to you at the door and cry. Others wave a cheery goodbye and are happy with a quick kiss. To be honest, both can be painful for parents! When my son started school, we had no tears, no demands for me to stay. Honestly, I wouldn't have minded – if just for one day.

Often how a child reacts depends not only on your reaction (if you're looking sad, they are more likely to mirror this), but also on their position in the family. First children frequently find it more difficult, as they feel as if they are being separated not just from their parents but from siblings at home. Younger children, on the other hand, look forward to joining their older brothers and sisters at school. We parents, however, often find it harder with our last! There's more on what to do if your child is finding it difficult to leave you in chapter 4.

"When Liam started school, he cried, and I think it was partly because he worried about what I was going to be doing at home with his little brother. He said he'd miss us both and was quite jealous about the thought that Ben would be having a nice day with me! But when Ben started school, he was so used to going there, that he just bounced off, excited that he'd be seeing Liam later. Their reactions were so different."

Emily

I was fine when my daughter started school. More than anything I felt proud because of how she was growing up. But when my son started school I felt quite sick and then I cried. However, I didn't let my son know. I thought that if he knew I was anxious, he would not just pick up on it, but get confused about how he should react. He might then have been torn between his great new adventure and his pathetic mother.

> If a parent is upset, we let them have a cup of tea in the secretary's office. We want to establish a routine as quickly as possible and if a parent stays in the classroom or shows they're upset, their child will never settle. The best thing to do is just walk out of the door. The child needs to learn that it's normal for the teachers to look after them, and that we're not mean and nasty!
>
> Louise Robinson, Headmistress of Merchant Taylors' Girls' School, Crosby

So, don't hang around in the morning for too long, but, even if you pointed out where the toilets were on an earlier visit, do make sure that you remind your child where they are before you go!

> When my daughter started school, she promptly wet her pants on day one – she didn't know where the toilets were and was too shy to ask the teacher. It would have been good to have had a drier start. . .
>
> Jenny

YOU WAVED GOODBYE: WHAT NOW?

On the very first day of school, I would not personally recommend leaving, alone, immediately. If you already know other parents at the school, arrange to meet up for a coffee or a walk in the park. The PTA may have set up a coffee morning for new parents, and if so, even if the idea fills you with dread, think about going as you will meet people in the same boat as yourself.

When your child starts school, you may be unaffected – or simply happy that you're at the next stage of parenthood. But many parents don't feel like that. Many feel emotional, especially if it's their only – or last – child, and some feel absolutely drained and bereft. So how can you help relieve those feelings?

> " When my youngest started school, he sat in his chair and looked so vulnerable I had to leave the room as I just could not stop the tears. I went into work feeling quite embarrassed until a colleague told me that she had felt the same way when her youngest started school. It's a whole new phase in life, part of the growing up process – for us as well as the kids. "
>
> Tina

The most important thing to realise is that you're not alone. There are thousands of us who feel strangely lost when our child hops off into the (beginning of the) adult world. If you don't work (or if you work a few days a week) then the days can seem really long. But don't rush to fill them straight away. You may well be suffering from empty-nest syndrome. Yes, I know it sounds strange, but it's true.

> " I couldn't believe how wobbly I was when my youngest started. The house seemed so quiet – even with the radio on – and, although it sounds dramatic, it was as if I'd lost my raison d'être. For almost seven years, I'd been a mum and now

it was as if I wasn't needed. I think I almost got depressed. ”

Lisa, mother of four

Empty-nest syndrome was so termed to explain the loss and sadness that many parents experience when their children no longer live with them or need day-to-day care. It's very common, usually when children leave home for university. But it can strike at any age.

“ Parenting is a constant letting-go. From the moment you play peek-a-boo with your child, you've started them off being independent and letting them know that you won't always be there. Feeling sad is common at any stage. There's no right and wrong about it. ”

Sue Atkins, parenting expert

What you need to do is take stock. We all neglect ourselves when we have young children, but now you can put the time to good use (start swimming, take up yoga, volunteer, do some part-time work, meet up with friends), take it slowly and decide what's best for you.

Of course, many parents have other children at home to keep them busy. You should be warned that younger children may miss their older siblings, but take heart that they may also meet their future friends during school pick-ups for older siblings. I met my best friend at primary school when we were in our prams (her sister was in the same class as my brother).

So, school has begun. Remember to turn up on time at the end of the day (children hate being the last to be picked up) and (truly important, this one) bring an after-school snack with you. Now, other than the rush of early mornings, the hell of the school run and meeting far too many new parents and children, what's next?

4

The first term

So, the first day is over and the rest of the term, and year, stretches out before you and your child. What do you need to know?

HE'S CRYING: WHAT CAN YOU DO?

It is truly awful to leave a crying child at school in the mornings. But most people (especially teachers) agree that it has to be done. After all, your child is in the hands of professionals and you need to trust them. "It's always good to get rid of the parents," confided one headteacher to me, while another experienced Reception class teacher added, "I have never had a child who didn't settle after his or her parents left."

> "It sounds horrible to say that we just want parents to go, but it's far better for the child and their settling in if the parents do just that. If you are happy for us to grab the child and whizz off then it makes everything easier in the long run."
>
> Ruth Vered, Reception class teacher

That, of course, is all well and good. But the reality is that it can be emotionally draining to have an unhappy child grabbing onto your knees each morning, especially if they haven't shown behaviour like this before.

> "Jamie was always very happy at nursery and has never been a particularly clingy child. That's why it was so hard when he cried each time I took him to school. It lasted for a few months and I found it such an awful experience – even when the teachers told me that he was fine soon after I had gone. I almost had to peel him off me every day and found it totally exhausting."
>
> Trudi, mother of Jamie aged 5 and Tom aged 9

Not only is going through all this very tiring, but it can also make you doubt your parenting skills. However, be assured that you shouldn't feel guilty. Children across the ages have cried when separated from their mums or dads. It will pass (eventually) but here are some ways to deal with it.

Just go

Top of the list, of course, is to disappear as soon as you can, and ignore your child's tears. Many teachers say this helps to establish a routine as quickly as possible. They argue that having a parent hanging around not only means their child won't settle, but upsets other children (then they want their mummies too). It also, they argue, sets up an expectation that the parent will stay if the child cries hard enough (a pattern of negative behaviour that can be very hard to shift).

If you can face running away, despite the tears, then this may be the solution for you. You could always ring the school office a little later in the day to check that everything has worked out all right. It nearly always will have.

But (and you knew there was a "but", didn't you?) this doesn't work for every child. True, I've spoken to a lot of teachers, and they have all said that it works "9 out of 10 times" or "almost all the time". But what if your child is the other one? I've heard tales of children who sprint after their disappearing parents and are inconsolable afterwards.

If you are planning to follow the "just go" line, then it might be more sensible to have a proper plan, rather than a simple vanishing act. Whatever you do, stick to what you've told your child in advance.

Don't say that you will wait and say goodbye, and then not do it. This could inflame the situation – making your child feel even more insecure the next day. Instead, tell your child exactly what you are going to do – whether it is that you will take him into the classroom, give him a kiss and then go, or that you will wait for him to seem happy and then leave, without an extra goodbye. You need him to feel safe.

Some children do have real separation anxiety and genuinely fear that something will happen to their parents (or even to themselves) while they are at school. You will probably know already if you have one of these children, because they will have reacted similarly when left at nursery.

> "Lots of children feel anxiety about separation and some of them feel it in an extreme way. They worry that bad things will happen to them or their parents – that they will get lost or taken, or that their mother might be in a car crash whilst they are at school. The key thing is for them to face their fears, and to learn that nothing bad actually happens.
> Lucy Willetts, clinical psychologist and expert in childhood anxiety"

If your child does have severe anxiety, then you need to agree a plan and be positive in your approach. Break the separation down into gradual steps. For example, you could say that you will bring your child in, hang his coat up, and wait for class to begin. Then, after a few days, you explain that while you will hang the coat up, you won't stay until class begins. Then you could suggest simply bringing your child into the classroom. Take it all in small steps.

Distraction

This is also a good option. It's something we've all done ever since our children were small – stopping a tantrum or tears by bringing out a toy or giving them a job to do.

"I found that distraction worked a treat. I would take Sanjay into the classroom and he would hold onto my knees for dear life. However, if I pointed out the Lego or suggested him going to find a friend and drawing a picture, I found that he soon cheered up. After about a week I would ask him what he was going to do when he entered the classroom and he actually became excited! I couldn't believe the change."

Nishi, mother of Sanjay, aged 4

Stay for a while

Not *all* teachers will want you to go straightaway, so if you are having problems, find out what your school's policy is.

"Every teacher has a thought about this, but I want the parents to come into the classroom and for the separation to happen gradually. I think it's lovely if the mum or dad reads a book with their child when they come in and then goes when they feel the child is ready. ”

Tanja Perez-Williams, Reception class teacher

“ Danny did cry and cling a couple of times in Reception. I stayed for about 20 or so minutes each time. Then the teacher, once she had got the other kids settled in, came over and took him to be with his friends or to do an activity. He was still crying when I said goodbye, but they kindly rang me half an hour later to say he was fine. ”

Joanna, mother of Danny, aged 5

Stick it to them!

Children of this stage (and even older ones) often like charts, at least if they have a reward at the end. It often works well if you suggest a star or sticker each time a child goes into the classroom nicely. Build this up, so that if they do a week's worth, they will get a good treat.

Disappear before drop-off

Sometimes children misbehave with their mums, but not with anyone else. If you organise some (hopefully temporary) help, then that may prove to be a breakthrough.

“ You can set up a vicious cycle, where the child dreads going to school and separating from his mum, and so the mum also begins to dreads it. The child picks up on that anxiety. It might be that if the dad or a friend can take them, it would be easier for the child. It's not that the child is playing up, but it means that they can separate from mum at home, which might be easier to manage and less distressing for the child.

Lucy Willetts, clinical psychologist and expert in childhood anxiety ”

Remind them of you during the day

“ For both the kids I used to put a memory of me in their pocket. So whenever they felt sad, they had a reminder of me, a bracelet, a watch, a badge, something of mine, so they felt they had a bit of me with them for the day. A note in a lunchbox can really help too.

Juliette, mother of three children aged 10, 7 and 4 ”

Suggest crying even more (it sounds mad, but it could just work)

“ I had major problems last year with tears/clinginess at the school gate from my youngest, but I fixed it by using reverse psychology. I told her to cry as much as she possibly could, and she ended up in fits of giggles. I was at my wits' end and desperate to break the pattern! I'm so pleased it worked.

Fiona Joseph, mother of two

He's not crying: what does that mean?

Neither of my children cried when I took them to school. And that's normal too. Not every child goes to pieces when they face something new. Some find it exciting. Others are simply unfazed.

Be assured that not having a crying child is truly great and is simply one less thing to worry about! It means your child is happy and secure, and doesn't have any fears that you won't be there to see him at the end of the day.

OTHER EARLY-MORNING ADVICE

I have lost count of the number of teachers who have said that their lives would be so much easier if parents didn't hang around chatting with other mums just outside the classroom. It may seem like a reasonable thing to do – why shouldn't you speak to your new friends? – but it can wreak havoc with the children. After all, they've just said goodbye. Now they need you to go out of eyeshot.

And a warning: while you may crack the clinginess during the first term, the problem can always rear its ugly head again. I'm afraid that after holidays, the holding on and crying can start once more. So, be prepared to go back into action with whichever plan worked best for you.

SOCIALISING OUT OF SCHOOL IN THE FIRST TERM

By the time your first child starts school, you'll have been a parent for a number of years and become used to organising a calendar for your youngster (often a calendar which is far busier than yours). So it may come as a surprise that once your child starts school, my advice is not to arrange playdates straight away. Negotiating a new environment can be exhausting and your child will probably be tired after a long school day. Don't overwhelm him with lots of after-school activities or arrangements. He'll need time to relax.

> "My son comes home very tired, which is strange because he was doing full days in nursery before. I don't know if it's because school is so much more stimulating, or because there are lots more children there, but it's obvious he needs to have a rest afterwards.
>
> Mark, father of a daughter aged 6 and a son aged 4"

It's strange but true that even if your child has gone to nursery, he will probably feel worn out after starting school. So, cut out the after-school ballet or swimming, at least for the first term, and restrict playdates to one or two a week (even if you are itching to put together a whole new roster of friends for you and your child).

> “My son was so shattered when he started school he didn't want to do anything afterwards. He was sobbing with tiredness.
> Ellen Arnison, mother of three boys, aged 10, 8 and 14 months”

The tiredness does, of course, differ from child to child, so (if you trust them!) do follow your child's lead. My son was exhausted after school and told me that he didn't want too many playdates. My daughter, however, has never needed much sleep and rarely feels tired. When she was in Reception, she was keen to invite her new friends to play and I was happy to do so because it seemed to make no difference whatsoever to her energy levels. You may find that the tiredness is heavily dependent on how old your child is - autumn-born children often find it easier to keep on going.

One important thing to remember is that your child is not going to lose out if you don't arrange playdates as soon as you possibly can. At this age, children can be fickle and change their friends constantly. They will not end up friendless if you hold back on arrangements at the start.

> “When my daughter started school, she was completely wiped out for the first few weeks. She likes playdates, but I'm strict and am only allowing one a week. I don't believe in over-loading children and know that she's with her friends all day at school. Some people seem to feel that it's really important to bond out of school. I think it's nice, but not essential.
> Tamar, mother of two girls, aged 4 and 2”

Personally I would arrange playdates when you think your child is ready as it is a great way for to deepen friendships. But that opens up a new can of worms. . .

MAKING CONTACT

Some schools give out lists of parents' details, which makes arranging playdates exceptionally easy. This is often done via the PTA, so do contact them and see if this is done in your school. Many schools have PTA representatives (see pp. 139–141) in each class, so these "reps" could help to draw up such a list if one doesn't exist already.

> "Getting a class list organised with everyone's contact details was key. It made it so much easier to go through the list, ask the children who their friends were, and then be able to contact them to arrange playdates. I'm not sure how I'd have managed without it."
>
> Claire, mother of twins aged 5 and a son aged 2

If you don't have a list, you will have to resort to other ways in which to arrange playdates. The easiest, of course, is to go up to the relevant parent in the playground (this will require a little detective work, but shouldn't be too difficult). You could also write a little note and give it to the child in question to take home in his bookbag. Don't worry – it's not really that complicated!

Remember that your child does not need to be friends with everyone in his or her class. Every child is different, and while some will flit from child to child, others will form small groups quickly. You will have to go with your child on this one.

Your child might be particularly shy or have problems making friends. You can help by showing that *you* are ready to make friends yourself.

If you talk to other parents in the playground, then your child may realise that it's okay to speak to people he doesn't know too.

> "It's always about you and how you model things. If you are shy and hold back in new situations, your child will be like that too. They learn from you, so you need to notice how you behave, and you might have to change."
>
> Sue Atkins, parenting expert

There's more on playdates and your child's friendships on p. 105.

THE IMPORTANCE OF A GOOD SLEEP

It is crucial that your child gets enough sleep to cope with the school day and this may mean instituting a proper routine – supper, bath and bed. A child in Reception usually needs between 10 and 12 hours of sleep. If they don't get it, they can become anxious, behave badly and be less alert at school. This, of course, will affect their ability to learn.

> "Tiredness can really affect children – and I have often seen this in the classroom. As a parent, it's so important to make sure your child is getting enough sleep, especially when they're often physically and mentally exhausted after school."
>
> Tanja Perez-Williams, Reception class teacher

REALITY BITES

When school starts, if your child is not clinging onto your legs (and indeed, if he is), he will probably be excited. But after a month or so, this excitement may fade. School may be fun, but it's also no longer a novelty, and the teachers soon start sneaking in some proper work. The honeymoon period is over.

This may be when you may find that your child develops a reluctance to get up in the morning, or starts to talk about tummy aches or headaches. He may become unsettled on a Sunday evening or suddenly start being much clingier.

Whatever happens (within reason – there will be more on this later) YOU NEED TO CONTINUE TAKING YOUR CHILD TO SCHOOL! If he sees that there is an option of not going, he will dig his heels in and you may find it very difficult to get him to return.

Be aware that he may not be pretending when he says he has a bad tummy. Anxiety can be physical. Chat it through and work on the positives. If there are any specific problems, for example with other children, do talk about it with the teacher, and if necessary with the headteacher.

> "If you've got a concern, you should raise it, no matter how trivial you think it is, and regardless of how early in the term it is. We want to make sure we are doing the best for your child in school and we definitely want to hear if that's not happening.
> Louise Robinson, Headmistress of
> Merchant Taylors' Girls' School, Crosby"

TOILET TRIPS

What are the toilets like at your child's school? If you are lucky, they'll be clean and well stocked with toilet paper, soap and paper towels. If you're unlucky, they just won't be.

Young bladders and bowels don't necessarily stick to a rigid timetable, and most schools realise this, allowing children in Reception to go to the toilet whenever they like (as long as they put their hand up). Many schools actually have separate toilets for Reception-aged children. But the state of the school toilets can make a child worried about actually using them and can cause real problems.

Fortunately most primary school loos are pretty good, but that doesn't mean your child will be happy. You may find them hanging on all day and then rushing to the toilet as soon as you get home. Or you may find that they won't drink properly during the day in case they need the toilet. It's in your child's best interests for you to find this out – and to nip any possible problems in the bud. Here are some simple tips.

Find out what the school toilets are like and talk about them with your child

You may want to suggest that he wipes them with paper before sitting down and encourage him to tell the teacher if soap or toilet paper has run out (or if someone has blocked up a toilet by stuffing paper down – we all know it happens). Make sure he knows basic toilet etiquette (to flush, wash hands *with soap* and dry them) but do feel free to send your child in with tissues which he or she can use instead of toilet paper in an emergency (one mum I came across sends her children in with anti-bacterial gel too!).

Bring in a spare set of clothes

If your child does have an accident, he's going to need something to change into afterwards. Many schools don't offer spare clothes as a matter of course, so pop some underwear and a spare pair of trousers in a named carrier bag and hang it on your child's peg. It doesn't have to be uniform, although something that won't stand out is probably best. Don't put in his favourite trousers, or he may decide to have an accident just so he can put them on!

THE SOUND OF SILENCE

Isn't it strange that your chatty, friendly child goes so monosyllabic when asked about school? And just when you are feeling so curious about what he has been up to.

Children do not always want to share everything with their parents, and now they are big enough to go to school, many want to keep that part of their lives secret. After all, school is their domain. It can be hard for parents, but although I'd generally recommend you to go with it (you don't have much choice), there are a few ways to get at least some of that much coveted information about what's going on during your child's school day.

1) Don't ask too many questions. If anything is guaranteed to make them clam up, it's bombarding them with questions the moment they walk out of the classroom. Give them a bit of space and they may decide to talk to you later on (often when they are in the bath or getting ready for bed).
2) Give them something to eat. Grumpy children are rarely forthcoming. Once they have a bit of food inside them, they may be more open to questions.
3) Ask other children. Some children will say a lot more to their friends' parents than to their own.
4) Ask in a different way. Perhaps ask if there was something which made them laugh at school that day, or what the "best thing" was.
5) Talk about your day. It may encourage them to open up about theirs.

> "You could ask 'so was anybody naughty in school today?' Yes this is a bit mean, but children can be very enthusiastic when it comes to ratting on other people's misdemeanours. And then you can steer the conversation round to what else their day consisted of."
>
> Joanne Mallon, parenting expert and coach

Many schools have weekly newsletters. If yours does, then you can use it as a starting point for discussion ("I see you have been making collages this week at school. Did you use leaves? What colours were they?").

> "My daughter usually says 'nothing' or 'I don't know' if I ask her about school, as if school is over and done with, so why talk about it? I've learnt to live with it. Sometimes she opens up a bit later on in the day – usually when I'm on the phone and need her to be quiet!"
>
> Deborah

If you want to make sure you know what's going on in school, you must (yes, it's that fundamental) check your child's bag every day.

Far too often your child will be carrying around an empty bookbag, but every now and then, the teacher will give out a school letter and if you don't check the bag, a vital piece of correspondence may end up squashed under leaves and conkers for days on end. Some schools also send out emails, but the bookbag should always be your first port of call.

Once you receive dates for school events (from dressing up for children's book week to, er, dressing up for Egyptian Day), write them down straightaway on a calendar. That way your child won't be the one whose bad mummy or daddy has forgotten. . .

SURVIVING THE SCHOOL RUN

Getting a child to school every day requires a plan. It may be that you have a simple 10-minute walk from your house, or it could be that it's half an hour's drive. Whatever the distance or time taken, the school run can be a real shock if your child has just started school.

Who knew just how slow a child can be in the morning, that telling a child to hurry up doesn't work, and that the traffic gets about 1,000% worse during school drop-off and pick-up times?

The school run is a messy, ugly thing, accounting for a whopping proportion of rush-hour traffic (an estimated 18%) and causing horrible congestion around the school. It can also be a rather odd experience. I find that there is often a strange panic that you will make your children late, and that if this actually happens, you feel ashamed way beyond sense. This panic usually inspires me, not naturally a morning person, to rush the children so much that we end up arriving long before we need to. Getting somewhere early is not something I carry over into the rest of my life, but perhaps it is indicative of the way we are with our kids – we allow ourselves to fail at things, but don't want to fail them.

So, if you want to make sure your kids don't get a black mark for lateness, you'll need to follow these tips. . .

Eight school-run tips

1) Get up earlier

This is pretty self-explanatory. It simply means you leave yourself more time to do everything.

> “My son doesn’t like being under a time pressure in the mornings. We’ve found that it actually makes him take longer if we try to hurry him up and shout things like ‘come on, we’re late’. Instead we need to let him feel he’s in control by getting him up a bit earlier. Then he can take it at his pace.
> Mark, father of a daughter aged 6 and a son aged 4”

2) Be organised

Organisation is key, so lay out clothes and pack school bags the night before, and make packed lunches to put in the fridge. You may not have time to start buttering sandwiches in the morning.

3) Always check

Don’t assume that your child has got out of bed just because you went in there and told him to “get up now” 20 minutes earlier.

4) Use bribery

Whether it’s a sticker chart or a treat after school, let your kids know that punctuality may result in a reward.

5) See it positively

This may be easier said than done, but my friend Julia says that the school run is one of the few times when she has all three children together in one place! This means she can use the time to talk to them, sing, do quizzes, or anything else which takes her fancy. Maybe it’s a mind-set thing. . .

6) Park and stride

This is something I now do with my children. In the mornings we park further away from the school and walk the last five to 10 minutes together. I enjoy this time, and find that I (usually) get less stressed about the parking. Of course, this plan does mean leaving extra time in the mornings, so it doesn't really help with that hectic get-out-of-the-house rush.

7) "Walking bus"

Parents have recently come up with the idea of a "walking bus", in which volunteers collect the children from designated "bus stops". If this appeals to you, then think about raising it with your school.

8) Walk

When I wrote about the school run on my blog, nearly every comment made suggested that parents should walk with their children to school instead. Of course, this isn't always practical, either for distance reasons, or time pressures (parents will need to walk back again too). But if you're keen to avoid driving and you want to get in some exercise, it's worth a try.

> "I think that most parents who drive their children to school do so because they have no option. It's not as if it's much fun to cram children into the back of the car. Yes, some parents are neurotic about how safe the streets are these days, but many live just too far away to walk."
>
> Alex, mother of two boys

Set up a rota

Another option, of course, is to car share or set up a rota with someone who lives nearby. Ask around at the school gate to see if there are other people who live locally and who are hoping not to drive to school every day.

However, be aware that the idea of the rota, while theoretically appealing (and helpful, particularly if you have to get to work) does not always go as planned. First, you have to share your car with children who aren't your own, and who you can't tell off if they are obnoxious. Second, these children will drive you mad (it's an unwritten rule), and third, you will find that they are never ready when you go to pick them up in the morning. It's probably still worth doing, but it's wise to be forewarned that it may not be a pleasure.

You will also need car seats for each child.

> "Don't be surprised if your first rota does not work out. But no matter how desperate you are to terminate it, never badmouth that mum or child as you don't know what will get back to them. Always stop rotas as diplomatically as possible. Remember that your child has to spend the rest of their school years with these children.
> Sophie"

Regressive behaviour

Children start school when they're very young and, even if they don't find it stressful, it's often exhausting for them, both mentally and physically. So, don't be surprised if they have a few little problems soon after starting school.

Anxiety, change and transition can all affect a child. You can help by trying to remain practical and not making a huge fuss. Of course, this can be easier said than done, and I wouldn't let the situation continue unchecked for months on end. But, as one mum said to me, cut them "some slack" for the first half-term or so. They'll soon get used to the change in routine and things will (hopefully!) get back to normal.

> "Sometimes children get more clingy and more babyish once they start school. They suck their thumbs or cling onto their teddy bears. It can be three steps forward and two steps back, at least at the beginning, but you need to support them."
>
> Sue Atkins, parenting expert

5

Navigating the school cliques for parents

Starting school can be scary and tiring for a 4-year-old. But let's not worry about the *children* for a moment. Because the school gate can be even scarier (though a little less tiring) for parents.

Remember what school was like in your day, with cliques and friendships so easily made and then shattered? Well, the same can happen when you go back to school and start all over again as a mother or father. Yes, even though you're decades older, it's time for you to make new friends too. After all, you're going to be stuck with these parents for the next seven years.

> "The good news is that there are plenty of other lovely people out there – sometimes you just have to look a bit harder to find them."
>
> Gillian, mother of Sam, 9 and Laura, 5

This chapter looks at how to make friends with fellow parents – because you can and (hopefully) you will.

It can be really stressful starting a new school and having to initiate conversation. Unless you are very outgoing, you may feel isolated sometimes and look around desperately for someone you know. Remember that most of us feel like this, and that there is nothing wrong with taking a deep breath and starting to chat about something completely random. A smile can also go a long way.

Many parents meet lifelong friends at the school gates, and it opens up a whole other world of potential confidants. However, all those new faces mean you need to tread carefully. The politics of the parental playground can be like a minefield.

MAKING FRIENDS

School opens up so many opportunities for friendships – for you as well as your child. It can be confusing, and even a little intimidating, but you should really try to see it positively as one of those times in your life (like going to university or starting a new job) when you have the opportunity to find yourself a new group of friends. Of course, if you're not a "glass half-full" type of person, you could just go with it as something inevitable (after all you can't really avoid seeing all these new faces, so you might as well make the most of it). You'll be meeting a new crowd, and hopefully some of them will be just your cup of tea.

Having a baby forces us to make new (and often valuable) friends, and this is also true when that baby grows up and starts school. I'm not saying that you have to become the life and soul of the party, but the school gate becomes a much more welcoming place when you've got friends there to gossip with.

“ You'll soon spot the kinds of people you want to be friends with. I can't say I like all the parents at school, but then I never liked all the girls when I was at school either. Give yourself time to find your way. And don't feel that you have to befriend the parents of each of your child's friends. ”

Julie, mother of two girls aged 10 and 5

It's definitely true that you don't have to be friends with everybody. That would be ridiculous. But you should be able to find a few people with whom you're on the same wavelength. And you shouldn't panic that your *child* may be left out if *you're* not everyone's best friend.

A quick warning

Your child starting school could unearth long-forgotten (or buried) bad memories of your school days, especially if you had a hard time with bullying or didn't quite fit in. Be careful not to project your feelings onto your children. This is about them, not you.

“ The biggest thing for parents to be aware of is how much of their stuff they bring to the party. We often need to hold back our initial instincts. It's not us going to school;it's our children. ”

Joanne Mallon, parenting expert and life coach

When your child starts school, you might not know anyone. Perhaps because of this, it can sometimes seem as if everyone else knows each other. This isn't true. We are all cowards at heart, so, if there *is* someone around that we know, we will tend to go and talk to them. The intention is not usually to exclude anyone, but this can happen, unintentionally.

> As a new mum, one of the things I am struggling with is the protocol regarding chatting to parents at the school gates. Lots of them already know each other from the school nursery or because they also have older kids in the school. Do I make friends among the mums and then hope our kids will also be friends, or shall I just hold back and wait to see who my son gets friendly with and hope I like the parents?
>
> Sara, mother of two sons aged 5 and 2

Last year, when my son started school, I found myself quite intimidated by the mums with younger babies, who seemed to have formed a kind of clique and were always talking to one another. I mentioned this to one of them, whom I knew anyway, and she told me (in a nice way, I assure you) that some of these mums found me and my friends (who knew each other already from having older children in school) a bit cliquey. Of course, this was not on purpose. We were just talking to people who had shared interests (in this case, younger or older children). Perhaps we are all intimidated by each other!

It is definitely true that making friends at school is simpler if you have things in common. Yes, we all have children, but it's easier to strike up a conversation with someone if there's more to it than that.

This is where babies in buggies, other parents dressed in tracksuits (if you're a gym bunny), or those of the same nationality can come in handy, especially at the beginning. After a while, you may find that these friendships change and that you have more in common with other parents (similar jobs, sons who love football, a penchant for foreign films). But during those early days, it's just good to talk to someone and not feel alone. Chatting to a parent you haven't met before also sets an extremely good example for your child. After all, if mummy or daddy can talk to someone they don't know, then he certainly can too.

In answer to Sara's question about whether to speak to mums she doesn't know (see p. 85), my advice would always be YES. Don't wait to be guided by your child. It's certainly true that you can't choose your child's friends (you can try, but it won't work), but *you* need friends too. If you're lucky, your friends will match theirs, but this won't always be the case, and you can't rely on it happening. In any case, it's also good to have friends whose children aren't particularly friendly with yours. It means you can talk about other things - not just the kids.

It's less stressful if your little one starts school with friends from nursery, or if he is the second or third in the family. This means you already know other parents and are used to the school set-up. If this is not the case for you, keep an open mind. Don't assume that these mums are all best-friends and unwilling to let others into their clique. Just go for it - it only means striking up a conversation.

IS THERE A PLAYGROUND MAFIA?

I try my best to dismiss the idea of a "playground mafia", even though people often talk about it, or of a school "Queen Bee" who rules the playground hive. I haven't found this to be particularly true, and get irritated when people assume it must be. After all, what better way to frighten new parents?

However it can, unfortunately, be true in particular schools. Some poor parents (mums *and* dads) have a really hard time at morning drop-off and pick-up. At their schools it seems that it really does matter where you live, what you wear or how clever or talented your child is.

"You will not believe how cliquey the playground is with the mums: it's horrendous. If you thought it was bitchy when you were at school, you'll get a real shock. Sometimes I think it's like some sort of social experiment, with posh mums sticking together and young mums sticking together. These different groups won't have anything to do with you!"
Jane, mother of two daughters

If you're experiencing this, you have a few choices. You can either look that bit harder for the mums like you, and although it may take time, you should be able to find them. Or you can give up, and rush in and out on school drop-off and pick-up (so you don't have to talk to anyone). What you decide to do will be up to you, but (and you won't be surprised by this), I'd recommend the former, or at least giving it a go.

Try to rise above any nasty gossip or tension and don't take horrible mums to heart. After all, remember that we are supposed to be showing *the kids* how to interact, and preferably how to be nice to one another. And if your child becomes friendly with the offspring of one of these scary mums, breathe deeply and arrange a playdate. You don't have to befriend the mum yourself.

"I truly believed that I was the ONLY person with school gate neurosis. The Mum Mafia could teach Marlon Brando a few tricks about psychological warfare. After years of waiting at the gates I've only once or twice had a decent conversation with a mum (I always avoid diet/leg wax/bitchy talk). So thanks to that one mum who told me she was retraining to be a lawyer. It made me feel human again. ”

Nicola, mother of three

A LONELY PLACE?

I said above that I'm lucky enough not to have experienced a "playground mafia". What I do find, however, is that the school gate or playground can be a lonely place.

When I go to pick up my children from school, I'm always hoping to see someone I know. What I want is someone I can easily go up to and chat with, so I'm not the sad, lonely one wandering around aimlessly. The playground – even at the most wonderful of schools – can be large and intimidating, and sometimes it seems as if everyone's friendly with everyone else, except you. It's like going back a decade or so, walking into the school common room and finding that your best friend isn't there to bolster you up.

I mentioned this to someone I bumped into out of school. She is one of those people who seems to know everyone, and is always surrounded by friends at the school pick-up. The funny thing is, she said that she felt that slight sense of panic too. Perhaps that's one of the most important things to remember: you're not alone. Millions of parents have had the same sinking feeling as you, we just hide it well!

“ I know some mums who try never to do the pick-up or just rush in, as late as possible, and then rush out again. I often end up standing on my own, but it does make me feel like I have no friends. And I do have friends – just not that many of them have children who go to the same school as my daughter! ”

Leila

> "When it comes to making friends, you may have to be more outgoing than you might like to be. Reception is the best time for making friends as everyone is new and lots of people don't know anybody. Just be brave."
>
> Joanne Mallon

Eight tips for making school gate friends

1) Don't gossip about other parents or children - at least not until you know them well enough! You're on dangerous territory if you bitch about particular children or parents because children's friendships change all the time.

2) Be open to new friends. Smile; be ready to make small-talk.

3) If you want to make new friends, think about getting involved. The PTA is one way to do this (see pp. 139–141) or you could suggest meeting for coffee with a group of mums. If you go to PTA meetings, you will meet mums across the school which can be a real asset (it's hard to be competitive with a parent who's got a child two or three years older than yours).

4) If you don't want to get too involved, at least go to some events. There will often be PTA "reps" in your class who may arrange a meal out or evening in a pub. These can be a good way to meet parents, without the children there to cause a distraction.

5) Don't feel under pressure. You don't need to be friends with everyone. Neither does your child.

6) Don't boast. Yes, your child may be wonderful, but share these thoughts with your husband and parents, not other mums and dads at school. Be tactful. Oh, and don't question others about how well their children are doing. There's no point and you'll just end up looking competitive (are you competitive mum?! See p. 92).

7) Try to include others and be helpful. If you are willing to be friendly, it will be reciprocated. Similarly, if you offer to help when another mum is in need, this could end up being very helpful to you later on.

> "Find out which kids live closest to you and take the time to meet their mums. Good parent relationships are invaluable, especially when you find you are too ill to do the school run, late picking up your child, or delayed at work."
> Dana, mother of a daughter aged 8

8) Give it time. You can't expect a friendship to be fully formed within days or even a few weeks. Remember your child is going to be at this school for seven years. You've got time.

> "Experience and the benefit of hindsight are wonderful things. I found that you make very strong friendships with your first child's year group. That's when you make a lot of effort to get to know people. With your second child, you know the ropes and have people to talk to. You can be calmer about it all."
> Rachel, mother of three sons aged 10, 7 and 3

If your child goes to school on a bus, you will miss the drama of the school gate. This may mean you will need to make more effort setting up playdates and that you will miss out on that school gate gossip (you are free to see this as either good or bad!).

PLAYGROUND POLITICS

As you've seen from the mention of the "playground mafia" above, life as an adult is not always as grown up as it should be. There's something about being back in the playground which seems to reignite behaviour which adults should have grown out of long ago. I'm afraid that you'll soon notice that the school gate has its own politics, that there are many different types of mums, and that status matters.

> "School gate politics are an important part of every parent's life, because you can feel very isolated if you're not included. It makes a real difference to be able to share experiences and it's very important in terms of talking through school issues."
> Margaret Morrissey from Parents Out Loud

Depending on what school you go to, your playground may have a whole variety of parents on offer. You'll roll up in the morning, children in tow, to find pushy mums and laid-back mums, Gina-Ford following mums and never-wanted-a-routine mums, trendy mums and hippy mums. And that's without mentioning the dads.

Personally, I would suggest that you don't get too hung up about this and that it's always better to have an open mind. However, some love the "school gate game", where you put parents into different categories. I'll show you how it works, but with one proviso, that you shouldn't take it all too seriously. IF I've got your word, then here are some examples.

Get ready for some stereotyping (but we all know that stereotypes often contain more than a grain of truth. . .)

The new mum

Yes, yes, at the beginning, all parents are new, but some are newer than others. You'll soon realise this, as those parents with children already in the school greet each other – and the teachers – as if they are old friends. This can be a little off-putting.

But there are benefits to being a new mum. New mums are optimistic, albeit nervous. They always turn up bright and early in the mornings and right on time at school pick-up, haven't had time to become cynical, and (hopefully) haven't judged any of the other mums yet.

The key to being a new mum is to enjoy it and take advantage of it. Only new mums can safely ask lots of questions and keep asking other mums their names (and the names of their children) until they remember them (but only for the first half-term or so, as otherwise it looks as if they have a dreadful memory).

However, give it about a term and you may see some cynicism creep in.

Some new mums seem to remain newer for longer. This is not to be recommended. While it's fine to be worried and gauche at the beginning, to continue to do so just winds up other parents and teachers. That can't be good.

Competitive mum

Oh, I have come across too many of these, and of so many different types (there are sub-categories here). I'm sure you will soon discover some choice examples as well.

Competitive mum can be competitive about so many things, from her own job, hairdresser or gym, to her precious child's abilities (from reading to maths; French horn to Chinese). And while you may be able to take her competitiveness about her house (so much nicer than yours), her holidays (so much hotter than yours), and her husband (earns so much more than yours, sadly), it can get far too irritating when she tries to compete via the kids.

How to deal with her

What you need to do is *take competitive mum with a pinch of salt* and make other friends so you can bitch about her. Also, try not to get caught up in her game (even though it is delicious to point out that your child won the school art competition and not hers).

You need to be on the lookout for competitive mum as she can be sneaky – she is the type who looks through your child's bookbag just to see what level of reading book he is on. She often brings office politics into the school arena (she may have been, or could still be, a high-flier at work, and now sees her children as an extension of that pressurised environment).

Competitive mum is commonly found at private and the more over-subscribed state schools, and the danger is that she will destroy your self-confidence. What you need to do is hold back and NOT become like her (don't find yourself secretly rifling through playdate bookbags and don't be tempted into a tutor for your barely reading 4-year-old).

Competitive mum can be a very nice person, if you can get past the competitiveness. Just make sure you don't ever have conversations about your children's abilities or progress.

The PTA mum

Bright, breezy and ever so eager, the PTA mum will soon shame you into helping with school events. Some people are extremely rude about her, particularly if she's a little bit too enthusiastic, and she can, seemingly effortlessly, move into threatening mode and then onto "PTA members-only" clique mode. However, most PTA mums are, as well as being super-organised, simply keen to make a difference, and they often do jobs which the school really needs (setting up the school fête, for example) and which wouldn't happen otherwise.

How to deal with her

Applaud her dedication and get involved *if you want to and if you have time*. But whatever you do, don't let this mum sweet-talk you so much that you find yourself at school meetings every night. Your family won't thank you. . .

The bitter mum

This parent used to like the school, but now bitches about it *all the time*. This might be because her illusions of what an education should provide (all focussed on her child) have been shattered. Or it might be because she's got no other friends. But if you talk to her for too long, you'll soon find yourself becoming bitter too.

How to deal with her

While we all need a good moan sometimes, bitter mum makes the world a greyer place. Spend too much time with her and you'll soon be moaning about the staff, other parents and children all the time. This mum will ruin your day. Say hello by all means, but try not to become bosom buddies (say no to those morning coffee suggestions). And if you feel very strongly about an issue at school, why not take it up with the staff, rather than expend too much energy talking about it with other parents.

The avoid-at-all-costs mum

You'll soon unearth this mum. She'll be standing alone and you'll go and talk to her, glad to have someone to speak to when you don't know many people yet. But then she will never stop talking, attach herself to you like a limpet and try to take over your life.

How to deal with her

You need to step back and extract yourself. And then make sure you have cover for the next time she comes near. . .

The mum-of-the-difficult-child mum

We are all very sorry for this mum, and she doesn't have an easy life. After all, it's not her fault that her child has problems (unless she is the cause, in which case she may well deserve her own Scary mum, category).

How to deal with her

Talk to her! This mum needs support and to know that she is not alone. A kind word doesn't mean your children need to become best friends.

However, while it's true that people feel a bit sorry for her, this won't necessarily extend to inviting her child over to play.

The kind-of-useless-but-pleasant mum

This is the mum who forgets everything, but who is so well-meaning, you can't dislike her. She turns up late on a daily basis, and has a remarkably bad memory.

How to deal with her

You can't, but that's no bad thing. This mum will make you feel good about remembering PE kits or Red Nose Day, because she will have forgotten. However, don't rely on her for playdates, unless you want an urgent call from the school about your apparently abandoned child!

The school governor mum

This mum has moved on from the world of the PTA and is, let me try to say this politely, sometimes a little snooty. She means to be open and welcoming to everyone, but when you bring up issues about the school, she has an uncanny ability to make you feel small, while simultaneously letting you know how busy she is with "school matters".

How to deal with her

Contact her by all means and even befriend her if you like. But be prepared for lots of comments about her busy life and name dropping of the school staff (they're all on first name terms, don't you know?)

The very strange mum

You simply won't understand this mum. She won't ever speak to you, her child won't turn up to anything (birthday parties, after-school clubs), and although the years may roll by and your children will see each other every day, you'll find you know nothing about her (including, perhaps, her name).

How to deal with her

You've got me on this one. After four years of one of these, I still have absolutely no idea (but we still invite her daughter to every birthday party we have - and never get a reply either way). If you have any ideas or tips, feel free to let me know.

The super mum

This mum seems to find nothing an effort. She's like headgirl and headteacher wrapped into one - with a top job, at least three children, and a remarkable ability to come to school events, help out when needed, and have well-adjusted children. She also looks good and never appears to be rushing. It should be enough to make you sick, but you'll probably find that you secretly admire her and want to be her friend. Mind you, she does seem more engrossed in her Blackberry than talking to you. . .

How to deal with her

You know what? Appearances aren't always what they seem. Super mum may have a good temperament, but she also has a lot of help behind the scenes (as you'll soon tell if your children become friends and are looked after by the full-time nanny). She may be difficult to befriend, because she knows so many people, but you can have a go. Just don't be disappointed if it's not reciprocated.

The gorgeous mum (sometimes known as yummy mummy)

Any of the mums can be gorgeous - even you. Although some people like to stereotype them as the kind of people who take oodles of time to look brilliant every morning, some of the most gorgeous women at the school gates are naturally beautiful (yep, it can make you green with envy).

How to deal with her

Don't lump all gorgeous mums in together. Some may spend hours perfecting their glossy manes, and this may not endear them to you.

But others may have good genes, nice children, and could even become your friend. They are a perfect example of why you shouldn't judge people by their looks.

When my daughter was in Reception, she told me that she wanted a particular girl to come and play. I rang the mum up (I had no idea who she was, but got her number from the class sheet) and we had a lovely chat. When I met her, I couldn't believe how absolutely gorgeous she was. I think I might have been too intimidated to speak to her if we had met at the school gate, but now, four years on, we are really good friends. How stupid I would have been if her sunglasses and model looks had put me off!

Despite that story, some of these yummy mummies can be a real handful. This less appealing version is obsessed with fashion, only speaks to the other equally gorgeous mums, and never wears the same clothes twice!

The part-time mum

Er, hello! This is me. I'm the trying-to-do-everything mum, from dropping off and picking up, to slotting in working/cooking/ playdates etc.

I like to think that I'm pretty harmless, but I know that I can often seem stressed, and rushed.

How to deal with her

Befriend me. Offer to help when I'm really busy and I'll reciprocate. Please don't look down on me because I can't volunteer for everything. My life is just holding itself together as it is.

As you can tell, there are so many school gate mums (I haven't even mentioned the hippy mum or the sporty mums who have their own netball team) and I'm sure you'll soon find some of your own. All their children will be mixing with yours, and above all, you need to remember that this will be the case for the next seven years. When you start, you are all in the same boat, so you may as well make an effort, even if you are shy.

I found it funny when the daughter of the trendiest, coolest, sexiest mum in the class became best friends with the daughter of the mum-who-will-not-wear-make-up. But as the children got friendlier, the mums gave each other a chance too. It was a lesson learnt. You should be open to each other, and not be too quick to judge.

School gate dads

Pity the dads. They often find the school drop-off, pick-up routine even worse than the mums, probably because they are fewer in number. For some reason, many women won't even acknowledge these dads – often those who work from home or take the main burden of childcare – as if they don't have much in common. Well ladies, you're wrong. You all have school-aged children.

> “The paranoia is incredible. Most of the mums seemed to think I was a weirdo for picking my kids up. In the end I always made sure I was talking on the mobile so I wouldn't even have to attempt to make polite conversation.”
>
> Tony, father of two girls, aged 6 and 4

Here's another eye-opening comment – hopefully it will make you see things from a different angle.

> “You should try being a house-husband. The playground 'mafia' is not a fiction for me. I feel really sad for my son knowing that he isn't invited round for tea or to play. I have given up counting all the times I have tried to get his friends in the class to come round. I've even signed him up for the same after-school activities as his friends and spoken to the mothers there. But they always treat me like

I'm a paedophile or as if I'm talking to them because I fancy them. ”

Ian, father of a son aged 6

THE WORKING/NON-WORKING DIVIDE

As if a multitude of school gate mums (and dads) aren't enough, they can all be divided further into two camps. You'll probably recognise them, but it's wise to be sensitive to both sides, if you can.

The working and non-working mums will moan about each other, just as (some) breastfeeding/non-breastfeeding mothers judged each other four years earlier. Both feel they are doing the best for their children. And who knows? They may both be right.

“ At my son's primary school, the working mums were too busy juggling their lives to get into little cliques – but would happily cover for each other, which was nice. The yummy mummies were quite scary and over-groomed, and many looked down on the working mums – but we were too busy to notice. ”

"Another mum"

How to deal with the divide

The truth is that both "sides" have lovely, and not-so-lovely members. Yes, it may drive you mad that the biggest decision in some mum's lives appears to be whether to go to the gym or the local coffee shop, but you don't actually know what else they might be up to in the day. It's wise not to start making generalisations, or bitching, until you have actually got to know some of the mums better.

Take note of the fact that it may not really be an intentional working mum/non-working mum divide. It may just be that it's easier to speak to people you see every day.

> "I can remember dreading the school gate. I worked full time so I really didn't have time to stay and chat to the other mums, and it seemed to me that they all knew each other really well. They would stand chatting in a huddle, while I would be on my own waiting for the bell to ring. Gradually, by getting involved in the PTA, I started to get to know the other mums and made some quite good friends. But there were still times when I was aware that because I was a working mum I was very much an outsider. To me it felt as though the non-working mums were in a sort of clique. But I was also aware that if my child was to form friendships with theirs, I needed to be as friendly as possible at every opportunity."
>
> Liz Jarvis, parent blogger and mum

It's certainly the case that some working mothers seem to prioritise work above everything else (I said some), but many others feel incredibly hassled and guilty about working, so don't rub in the fact that they can't be at every event or school pick-up. I've found that working mums are very good at volunteering for everything they can (and they sometimes wonder why the non-working mums don't seem as dedicated).

It can also be true that some stay at home mums (or SAHMs) look down upon their working-mum counterparts and judge them for not being available for every playdate or coffee morning.

However, you can't lump all the SAHMs together either. Many feel they have a lot of spare time now their kids are a bit older and are keen to help out at school. Others never volunteer, but this may be for a myriad of reasons (and not because they're lazy).

> "The thing is, you just don't know what's happening in someone else's life. You can't assume that because someone doesn't work, they have loads of spare time. They may have that time filled with all kinds of things, from volunteering, to caring for an ill relative.
>
> Debbie, mother of three children, aged 7, 5 and 2"

WE AREN'T THAT DIFFERENT REALLY

Although the school gate may become a major part of your day, try not to take it too seriously. One survey, by MumPoll.com, looked at the issue and found that 78% of respondents agreed that their one-upmanship at their school was "ridiculous", but admitted that they just couldn't help themselves. I have some sympathy for this. I know that even the nicest parent (as you'll have seen from the tongue-in-cheek stereotypes above) sometimes succumbs to a little bit of showing off about their offspring.

The research suggested that we are all in a rush for our children to achieve - whether it's to walk quickly or read earlier than anyone else (not that these milestones actually prove to be that important in the long-run). More than a third of those asked said that they talk up their children's successes in the classroom.

Is this really that surprising? There's a fine line between parental pride and bragging - and it's one we need to try hard not to cross. It can be really thoughtless to go on about your child's reading ability to a parent whose child is struggling. But it's perfectly acceptable to smile when your little one reads a road sign on his own – in front of another parent. Call me old-fashioned, but aren't we mums on the same team?

> "For 30 years I have been asked about school gate rivalry. It always has been and will always be! We are mums, we are human and it actually keeps some of us going. It's not bad to be proud of your children. Blink and the children will have grown and it will all be over, so enjoy and remember every minute."
>
> Margaret Morrissey, Parents Out Loud

Yes, you may be judged, but then again, you may not. At my children's school, I don't feel as if I am being judged, whether for my parenting skills or what I wear. And I don't judge other mums either. I've also made some really good new friends – and am sure you will.

After all, there is something to be said for having a group of people around you who understand your life and the joys – and difficulties – of having small children.

6

Navigating the school cliques for children

School is not just about learning (in fact, I've hardly mentioned learning at all so far – it will be discussed in detail in chapter 8). It is also about socialisation, making friends and growing up.

Friends are one of the best things about going to school. They can help your child feel really positive about their school experience, and also make the school day more fun.

Children can make and change friends easily. Be aware that friends may come and go depending on such simple things as which table he is on or which group your child is put into at school. If they see the same children all the time because they are seated together, they may build up strong – or apparently strong – ties. Yet if the tables are subsequently jiggled around, they may start talking about different children altogether.

I sometimes feel that adults can be rather patronising to children when it comes to friendships. Almost every expert I've ever spoken to has said that young children's friendships change constantly and that your child will proclaim him or herself to be "best" friends with huge numbers of people whilst at school.

However, all children are different and, at least in my experience, many of them make friends in Reception and keep them all the way into Year 6. As I mentioned before, I met my best friend before I even started school and we were very close until we went to different secondary schools, aged 11. My daughter is now nearly 9, and I'd say that most of the "best friends" (BFs) in her class, got together in Reception. Some of them even came in from nursery as BFs. In other words, school friendships can be long-lasting, so you need to give your child the best opportunity to develop these important relationships.

In this chapter, I will help you navigate the friendship minefield, a place littered with potential pitfalls. You only want the best for your child, but friendships, although important, can lead to tears as well as laughter. And as for playdates and birthday parties, well, they're hazardous too.

HOW CAN YOU HELP?

It's really important to encourage your child to make friends. You have a big role to play, and your child will use the skills he learns from you.

It's hugely important to act in a friendly manner yourself - even if you feel shy.

> "I had to work hard at making friends with parents so that we could arrange playdates for the children. It involved being really friendly and persevering with saying hello until eventually people warmed up. I asked the girls their advice for making friends, and they said they just went up to people and asked if they wanted to be their friend. For them it was so simple!"
> Claire, mother of twins aged 5 and a son aged 2

Friendships work best when children behave well to each other. So it's great if your child knows how to share (you can easily encourage this at home) and also if you give him ideas for how to deal with a particular situation (for example, not to hit back if someone hits him). It's also useful if you have the kind of child that other parents will want to invite round! This means encouraging good manners (lots of "please" and "thank yous") and helping them to improve their eating habits (all parents love entertaining a child who eats. My daughter has garnered plaudits by having a large and indiscriminate appetite).

The other way you can help to encourage friendships is by organising playdates. I think playdates are an invaluable way for friendships to deepen, especially as some children (often those who are on the shy side) prefer a one-to-one encounter rather than a big group. Playing with a child after school can also help to cement a move from acquaintances to friends.

> "Your job as a parent is to make sure your children have the confidence to make friends for themselves. If you have a super shy child who lacks confidence, be extremely pro-active about play dates. Sometimes helping in class is a good way to suss out the dynamics and work out who might be the right person to have over for tea."
>
> Barbara, mother of three children aged 8, 7 and 4

If you're not sure who your child plays with, don't worry, as there are various ways around this. One is to simply ask him and then trust the name he comes up with (you will probably know your own child on this one and whether he is likely to say someone he actually plays with or a random name). You should also listen very carefully to see if he ever mentions another child's name. You can also ask the teacher.

> "Parents often ask about friendships. They want to know who their child plays with and if they are happy. We carry out lots of observations of the children and note down who they play with."
>
> Ruth Vered, Reception class teacher

> "With Danny, it was the teacher who told me that he was quiet and played with another quiet little boy, William. So I made a point of getting to know William's mum and arranging a playdate. They are still best friends now, and luckily I am still friends with his mum!"
>
> Joanna, mother of Danny, aged 5

A helping hand

Many schools have aids for helping children make friends. These may include a friendship bench (where a child can sit if he has no one to play with) or a buddy system, whereby older children befriend specific younger ones so they always have someone to go to in the playground. It's definitely worth finding out if your school has these, as you can then encourage your child to make use of them if they need to.

> "The friendship bench was a godsend when my son started school. He would sit on it and said someone

always came up to him to make sure he was okay.
Karen, mother of a daughter aged 8 and a son aged 7 ”

CLIQUES FOR CHILDREN

Much as it might make your heart sink, children can form cliques, even in primary school. And although these don't tend to be hard and fast, especially right at the beginning, it's just as well to be aware of them.

When my son started school, he soon got together with a group of four other boys and stuck with them throughout the rest of the year. I couldn't work out the bond until I realised that these boys all loved creative games and that none of them were into either football or Star Wars!

“ Clique-wise, for primary school kids, I think it has a lot to do with interests – football, for example, or after-school clubs (there are a group of girls in Sanjay's class who hang out because they all do ballet after school together). With boys it seems to be that if they share the same interests in toys (with us it was Transformers and then Toy Story), then that decides who they play with too.
Nisha, mother of Sanjay, aged 4 ”

One thing you may notice is how different a child's interests are depending on their position in the family. Those with older brothers may be more interested in "grown-up" things like Star Wars (although they have probably never seen the film) or particular television programmes. Those with younger siblings may still be happy to sit and watch CBeebies.

FRIENDSHIP GROUPS

If there is just one maxim when it comes to school and friends, it's that your child's choice of friend is not up to you. Don't decide which parents you do or don't like and then try and foist their child upon yours. It will almost certainly backfire.

> "Have some faith in the way your child picks their friends – they do know what they are doing, and when they are working out who to be friends with they are aware if someone is nice or not. If you don't 'approve' you can socially engineer a bit and reduce playdates down. Just don't make a big thing of it."
>
> Petra, mother of two daughters

At first, it may be tempting to try to persuade your child to invite over children that you already know, or be thrilled when your son or daughter befriends a delightful child with beautiful manners and a lovely family. But if he then decides he doesn't actually want to be friends with this child any more, don't get stressed about it: 4 and 5-year-olds can be fickle. They have a whole class to check out.

> "Last year my daughter was in Reception and right at the end of the summer term I remember the teaching assistant telling me that she asked one child to 'please go and give this to John' (John being another child in the same class). The child replied, 'Who is John?' I thought that demonstrated beautifully how in Reception the kids are in their own little world and although they are surrounded by 29 other children every day it really doesn't mean

they know everyone or need to be friendly with them all.

Emma, mother of two girls, aged 5 and 7 ”

Be aware that some children find it difficult when their "new best friend" begins to play with another child. It's important to make sure that your child understands that everyone is allowed more than one friend.

At some schools, many of the children know each other before they start Reception. They may have been in the school's nursery, and so already formed strong bonds, or they may have come from another nursery together, and then stuck together for familiarity's sake. At the beginning this can be hard on those parents and children who didn't know each other before. But while some children then remain together throughout the school year and beyond, others soon go off and find other like-minded people to have fun with. However, some children find the change from nursery to Reception hard going.

“ It's very normal for it to take time for a child to adjust from nursery to school. A lot of children find it hard to cope with change. Sometimes they can be quite possessive about nursery friendships.

Joanne Mallon, parenting expert and coach ”

“ With my younger daughter, I found that she was a bit upset when her friends from nursery wanted to play different things or with different people. I asked her if she would talk to one extra person a week, and she now has new friends.

Liz, mother of two daughters, aged 7 and 4 ”

COMMON FRIENDSHIP PROBLEMS

My child doesn't want a best friend

Some children are desperate for one person they can click with and who helps them feel secure. Others don't want - or need - this, and like to play with different children at different times.

As your child grows up, you have to learn to trust them to do what's right for them. Just because you had a best friend at school doesn't meant your child will be the same.

> "My little girl had a tough time when she arrived at school with her best friend. Mine was much more outgoing than her friend, so made new friends very easily. Her best friend was devastated and mine felt very tied and restricted by the friendship. It resulted in a lot of tears and upset. Eventually the best friend caught up with her and they remain best friends after three years at nursery and four years of school.
>
> Angela, mother of a daughter aged 8 and a son aged 4"

My child seems a bit of a loner

He might be like you! Remember that your child may simply be a more solitary type of person. Perhaps he's a reader or a dreamer. It would be great if he played with other children sometimes, and you can help with this when he's small by organising playdates. If you're more concerned than that, you could also speak to the teacher to find out how your child behaves while in school.

However, I wouldn't worry too much. Instead, take account of your child's own attitude to all this. Is he happy simply doing his own thing or does he want more friends?

My child says he doesn't have any friends

This can almost break your heart. After all, what's worse than a child who tells his mum or dad that he doesn't have any friends and that nobody likes him? But before you spring into action, it's advisable to find out if this is actually true. Many children have claimed to have no friends, while a quick word with the teacher shows the opposite.

It could also be a matter of time.

> "It could just be a question of new term blues. Once your child has settled in and got to know their classmates better they may be much happier at school."
>
> Joanne Mallon

If your child is having difficulties, you can help by having friends over to play. For some reason, when a child is having a friend round after school, they usually play with him in school that day as well.

Another avenue worth considering is after-school activities (though remember at the beginning your child will be extremely tired). These can be a very good confidence booster.

> "You have to give opportunities for your child to shine and this may mean getting her confidence in another situation. Sign her up for swimming or judo

perhaps and let her grow and develop her self-esteem.
Louise Robinson, Headmistress of Merchant Taylors' Girls' School, Crosby ”

You could also try to show your child what a good friend is, and how a good friend acts – to be fun and helpful, and to have good ideas for games they can share.

“ My older boy is easy, confident, surrounded by friends. My younger one is not. It took me a long time to accept that they are just different and that my trying to foist friends he didn't want onto the younger one was counter-productive. Although children can be beastly, it's often best, as with dogs (also beastly), just to leave them to sort it out rather than hover over them.
Milla, mother of two boys ”

It's very difficult to make your child be friends with someone and these kinds of "fixed" friendships can often peter out.

There's more on dealing with shyness on pp. 214–217.

I don't like who my child is playing with

It's not always clear why a child picks another child to be friends with. Sometimes it may be shared interests. Other times it may be because of familiarity (they were at nursery together and then stuck with each other at school). At other times it may be because a particular child is charismatic or creative and comes up with great games to play.

While some parents may be very happy with the new friends their child has made, others may not be. Even 4 and 5-year-olds can be manipulative and unpleasant, and that's hard to deal with as a parent.

> "What can you do if your child gets into a group that he loves but you're not so happy about? Do you leave it, or avoid playdates with certain kids? Do you arrange lots of playdates hoping they get too much of each other? I have learnt that I just have to leave my son to make his friends, and just make sure I am there to guide him, listen to him, help him and understand him if things go wrong."
>
> Cathy, mother of two sons, aged 5 and 1

When your child is small, you can guide him when it comes to friends. You can suggest other people to play with and try to broaden out his friendship circle. And, if you are especially unhappy, you can talk to the teacher and suggest that she keeps an eye on the situation, or perhaps ask for some simple changes – for example, that your child and this child don't sit together at lunchtimes.

> "If your child is friendly with a child you don't like, don't feel pressured or obliged to invite that child back to play. You can control how often your child is around them. It's helpful to remember that you are your child's primary role model and that you are always teaching your child your important values, such as being generous, kind, tolerant, patient, and trustworthy and showing what a good friend is."
>
> Sue Atkins, parenting expert

> "Whenever either of my boys have any problems with school friends (which luckily isn't often) I go on the offensive and invite the other child home to play ASAP. That gives me the chance to a) see for myself what is going on (they might be little angels for the first 15 minutes, but after that, tend to revert to type) and b) make my own comments about what is and isn't acceptable behaviour in 'our' house."
>
> Clare, mother of two boys aged 7 and 4

If you are at all concerned that the behaviour is tipping over into bullying you need to address this with the school. There's more on bullying on p. 217.

My child sometimes falls out with his friends

Friendships can go wrong, particularly with girls, who can fall in and out of love very easily. The best advice I can give here is to support your child, but not to go wading in unless you feel it's unavoidable. Children can be surprisingly robust and capable of fixing friendship problems themselves. It's also better for their social development if they learn to sort out their own issues and don't always rely on you.

If your child is having a lot of problems with a friend at school, talk to his teacher BEFORE you talk to the other parent. The teacher will have an idea of what's going on, won't take sides, and could also help to encourage the children to play better (or even apart!)

I don't like the parents

This is much less important than you might think – especially if you don't invite parents over for playdates (see below for more on this). All you need to do is pick up your child, say thank you and go. It's your child who is making friends. This doesn't mean you need to befriend the parent of each child he chooses to see socially. You need only to be civil.

PLAYDATE ETIQUETTE

You'd be surprised how many issues there are when it comes to playdates. These include anything from how much you supervise (I say not too much, they'll have had organised activities all day in school and often want to do their own thing) to how many you should host (don't go overboard, it's not a competition). Some parents even worry about how tidy their house should be (you can make your own judgement on this!).

With or without mum or dad?

From my point of view, one of the joys of having your child go on a playdate is that you get some time either with your other children, or alone. In other words, I very rarely go. Of course, if I felt that it would help my child, I would accompany him or her, but my default position is to get them to go alone and have fun without me.

However, it's always worth checking whether you are *expected* to come along on a playdate. This can vary, not just from school to school, but from class to class, and you don't want to make a social faux pas when new friendships are being formed. Some parents prefer it if other parents come along. Some really don't!

Similarly, make it clear if you are expecting a parent – and other siblings – to come when you have a child round to your house. It may be that they want to come and make friends with you. Which is also allowed. . .

" I personally like to go on playdates, and always go when it's someone new. Brian can be quite shy, so I need to know if he's happy. And because he's an only child, it's nice for me to have a chat with a grown up. It's my way of making friends too. ”

Annie, mother of Brian, aged 4

Note that some parents - particularly those who are quiet and find it difficult making conversation - can get really stressed about having other parents round to their house. They may be fine with having the children round, but hate having to make conversation with adults they barely know.

If this sounds like you, my advice would definitely be to find out what's expected before you make up your mind not to host playdates. It might be that you simply suggest having the child round alone, or that you host a few children - and say to the parents that it might be just too chaotic with three or four mums there too! If you don't want to look too anti-social, suggest that the mum or dad comes in for a quick cup of tea before pick-up. Fifteen minutes is better than a couple of hours - you can just talk about the kids.

My child doesn't want to go on playdates

Some parents feel that there is a huge pressure to set up playdates, even if this isn't right for their child. In this case, you have to be - once again - your child's advocate, and explain the situation to others.

“ At first, my youngest son never wanted to go on playdates or to parties. He simply wasn't comfortable about going to other people's houses and found it stressful. My feeling was that he had to go to school, and he wasn't unhappy there, but he didn't have to go to parties or on playdates. There was no reason to cause him more stress, so we didn't, and he still made friends. Now he's a little older and fine about it.

Kate, mother of three, aged 11, 9 and 6

How many times can I say it? Each child is unique. Kate's youngest was completely different from her other two, who were always happy to visit other friend's houses. She gave him time, and left him to decide when he was ready. You might have to do that too.

Playdate pressure

It's true that there can sometimes be pressure - from children and other parents - to host playdates, and that this can be hard on parents.

I get the feeling that I'm a negligent mum because I'm not organising more opportunities for my kids to have friends round. It's difficult to fit it all in, when I'm working and the person who looks after my children when I'm not around isn't very happy about having others round to play. On my days off, I take the girls to swimming and ballet.

VK

As you'll have realised, I do think playdates are a wonderful thing for your child, but it doesn't mean you have to host them constantly. Perhaps you could try to have a child round every few weeks or months.

If you have someone else looking after your child (a grandparent, nanny or au pair), always ask if they are happy to host playdates on your behalf. And tell the parents of the child who is coming round if you are not going to be there.

But I simply don't want to host any playdates!

Not every parent wants to invite other children round to their house. This can be for a multitude of reasons. For example, you may feel too busy to organise another child coming round to play, or you may feel too shy or nervous to be the host.

Some parents feel they have to put on a bit of a show when they have other kids round - though this isn't necessary. They can get even more stressed about having to entertain the parents.

Tips to help a reluctant hostess

1) Suggest playdates on neutral territory. Kids love going out, so suggest taking your child and his friend to the park or soft play.
2) Do *a bit* of organisation. Don't over-organise on a playdate, just let the children get on with it. But when they're very little, you may need to supervise and you could make sure you have some things planned – *just in case*.
3) Don't worry too much about the food. Ask the parents in advance what their child eats. If they say that their son or daughter is fussy, ask what kind of food might appeal, usually something simple like pasta or fish fingers. Don't do anything elaborate. You're not trying to impress infant-aged children with your culinary skills. I always serve vegetables when kids come round, but I try not to get too stressed about children who won't eat anything with Vitamin C in it.

Timing is key

Always check what time you are expected to pick up your child - and make it clear roughly what time you expect a parent to pick up theirs.

If you have young children, you may want playdates to end at a reasonable time, say 6pm, so you can start the bedtime routine. However, your child may have befriended a youngest or only child who has a much later bedtime and whose mother thinks nothing of ambling along to pick them up at 7.30pm. This can become frustrating, so lay down guidelines early on.

I keep inviting over a child, but the parent doesn't reciprocate

This is another all too common parental refrain – and one which many of us have gone through. Your child makes good friends with another child and you invite him over. They have a great time. A few weeks later, your child says he would like to have this child over again. Should you invite him or should you wait for the original invitation to be reciprocated?

Oh, we parents are so paranoid! We really need to try harder not to get hung up on who has come to play and who hasn't. More often than not, there is no reason at all behind the fact that your child has not been invited back – it's not personal. Instead it could be that the mother in question is so busy she doesn't have time to think about organising playdates.

What you shouldn't do is worry that the other parent doesn't "like" you or your child. Busyness and oversight are far more likely reasons.

However, if this goes on for a while and your child is really keen to go to the other child's house, you may need to have a quick conversation mentioning this – something light-hearted along the lines of "Zach has come to us a few times now, but Sammy would love to come to your house to play one day if that's okay with you."

Note: If you have any fears about whether your child will be safe in another child's house, then don't send them there. Don't put your need for them to have friends above the necessity that they are safe.

THE BIG BIRTHDAY ISSUE

> “When my son got his first birthday invitation at school, it was from a child I didn't know at all. That's when I realised that the mother was obviously inviting the whole class – of 30! Apparently this is normal, but I couldn't believe it. My son is quite shy and wouldn't want a huge party and of course it makes it really expensive to have so many children.”
>
> DWS

These days children's parties can be obscenely expensive. Part of this is probably down to raised expectations among the kids: they may want an entertainer who could charge anything from £100 upwards for an hour of fun. But space is also a factor, and this has to, at least partly, be down to the "invite the whole class" mentality.

To be honest, the primary school party world is a bit of a nightmare. It can be like a military operation – sorting out venue, entertainment, food and going-home presents. And that's without keeping an eye on all the children.

But before you panic that you will be bankrupt before your child leaves school, take heed of the fact that the "big birthday issue" changes as your child moves up the school. Yes, it has become increasingly common for younger children to have whole-class parties. But as they grow older, they may want smaller, more exclusive affairs, just girls, or just boys.

> “It's an unwritten law that when a child is young, you invite the whole class to a party and foster a feeling of inclusivity. By Year 1 or 2 though, some of

the boys will want football parties and some of the girls will want princess parties. That's acceptable. It follows the natural pattern of the kids. ”

Rachel, mother of three boys, aged 10, 7 and 3

If you take a group of parents, some will argue that you simply must invite the whole class, others that you should stand up for yourself and tell your child to only pick a few children he really likes. Neither is "right" – there is no definitive answer here.

Some parents argue that having more children and bigger and better parties is just another way to ramp up competition at the school gate. However, it may just be that you think this is the perfect way for your child to meet his whole class, or that your child himself is a sociable little thing and doesn't want to upset anyone by missing them out.

One of the most pressing problems is that inviting everyone means large numbers. Most state schools have 30 children in a class. It's not easy to fit that many children into your house - and that's without worrying about mess and breakages, not to mention parents (in Reception, many parents accompany their children to parties and then expect drinks and food too). For many people, hosting vast numbers can be completely impractical.

“ We are full-time working parents on a tight budget in a two bed flat. The idea of throwing a party for 30 kids has just never been an option. My older daughter has never had more than six friends over, with homemade food and entertainment. I found the whole 'invite the class' birthday thing just added to the pressure and guilt that seems to come with being a mum. ”

Claire, mother of Chloe, 11, and Isabel, 5

So what can you do?

Decide what you can manage

Children will often ask for a whole-class party because they realise that means a huge number of presents, or because they've been to others. Don't even have this as an option if it's not right for you.

> "We have a simple rule – they can have as many guests as their age; only broken this year by a joint birthday party for the two of them. We've hired a whole swimming pool for £70."
>
> Andy

Do what's right for your child

It might be that your child wouldn't want a big party because they hate crowds. If that's the case, certainly don't have a big bash for everyone else's sake. Remember to ask your child what they would like for their party – don't make all the decisions yourself!

Either invite everyone or just invite a few

Don't miss a small number of children out – that's cruel.

Post invitations if you're not inviting everyone

You should also tell your child not to discuss the party in front of everyone at school.

Note: some schools say that invitations can only be given out on school premises if every child is invited.

Don't be offended if your child is not invited

Life's too short to worry about these things. It might be that although you invited the whole class, some children have parents who don't want to do this, or can't afford to. There's no need to judge them.

However, if your child hasn't been invited to the party of a good friend, I would suggest mentioning this (in a friendly way) to the parent. It could just be an oversight, and you won't want it to start eating you up (yes, we parents can get that worked up about events in our children's lives - you'll see).

Take note of the difficult child

This doesn't mean you don't invite him. However, if he's likely to be disruptive, speak to the parents beforehand and suggest that they stay and take responsibility for his behaviour.

Try not to let your child turn his party into a weapon

You'd be amazed at how many children do this, saying that others can or can't come to the party. Clamp down on this behaviour immediately if your child starts doing it. It can be really upsetting for a child who hasn't been invited, and confusing for a child who has received an invitation, but then thinks it has been revoked.

Organising the party

If you're inviting the whole class. . .

Only have them in your house if you've got the space and don't mind mess and breakages.

If not, then hire a venue. Check out places locally and compare prices: church halls are one good option, as are leisure centres (which sometimes offer swimming or soft play quite cheaply). Ask other parents for suggestions.

Think about sharing the party. Find out if any other children have birthdays the same time as yours and then you can split the costs.

" Our son had a joint party with a friend – halving the cost and meaning that the whole class was invited. We also asked parents to send only one present and then divided them up on a pot luck basis. I don't think it's good for children to get 30 presents at a time and this is one solution to that. ”

Annette from Cardiff

Don't over-cater

There's no need to go overboard with food for parties. You're not competing with other parents to become the next Nigella. Keep it simple – kids don't know the difference. Go for food which isn't too pricey (mini sausages or sandwiches, carrot sticks and chocolate crispies). Kids never eat that much at parties, so if you don't make too much, you won't be kicking yourself later. It's the food which often bumps up the price of parties, so if you can, do most of it yourself rather than buying it.

Make the rules clear

If you're short of space, ask parents not to bring siblings. Similarly, it's probably wise to ask how many parents are going to stay when the party is on. Remember that you will need to cater for this – both space-wise and with some food too.

Take bin-liners for afterwards

These come in incredibly handy, both for clearing up and for taking home the presents (but don't mix these bags up).

Helpers

If you're at a venue, try to have a dad around to assist – it's so helpful when little boys need to go to the toilet!

You might want to arrange to have a certain number of parents who stay, or (even better, as they won't simply be interested in their own child!) some other non-connected adults (siblings, parents, your best friend) to help you to serve and clear up.

Save the date!

There are nine children with January birthdays in my daughter's class. When it comes to their parties, you have to nip in quickly to take a date for your child (or contact all the relevant parents and sort it out between you). Feel free to do this some months in advance, or you may lose the date you want.

This is much easier if you have a class list. Such a list can also be used to see if other children have the same birthday as yours, so you can share a party.

Presents

Don't feel obliged to spend a fortune on presents although it's difficult to recommend a specific price as this differs from school to school and across the country.

> "I try to spend around £5 a birthday present. My tip would be to bulk buy – if you see something good in the sale, buy two or three of them and put them in a cupboard. Also, always remember to take the price off!"
>
> Julia, mother of two, aged 8 and 5

I personally feel that, although your child might love it, 30 presents is a ridiculous amount for one child. It makes sense for parents to club together and buy one bigger (and better) present, but that's something you would have to suggest yourself. Or you could ask for no presents at all (though your child may disagree!).

Party bags

The final big birthday issue is that of the dreaded party bags. I'm not a huge fan of these (the word "tat" comes to mind) and their contents (apart from the obligatory chocolates of course) nearly always end up in the bin soon after arriving at our house. They're also expensive, easily costing around £5 a bag, if you're not careful.

So, why not buck the trend? There are great alternatives to party bags, and you will be thanked (by parents, and hopefully, children too), if you go for them.

You could give out books as going-home presents (check out The Book People, www.thebookpeople.co.uk, or Red House, www.redhouse.co.uk, for great sets which can be split for going-home presents). One of my daughter's friends gave out hula hoops (not the crisps) at his party, which was fantastic - they were still being used over a year later. Another handed out skipping ropes and another gave out bulbs for planting.

> "One of the best parties I've been to had the children make their own party bags (well decorated paper ones). They also made a number of other craft items, which went into the bag to take home, and that was it. Kids had a great time and no plastic rubbish in sight."
>
> Emma, mum of three, aged 6, 4 and 2

Find out how birthdays are celebrated in school. Some children are expected to take in a cake or biscuits to mark the day (they'll be more about this in chapter 9 on food).

7

Dealing with the school

Once you have a child at school, your life changes, whether you want it to or not. If you thought you could get away with simply dropping your child off at the school gate each morning, think again.

Each school is a distinct organisation run by the staff and governors and with an army of parents behind the scenes. How much you get involved with school life is up to you, and depends on how many other demands you have. But one thing is true - you will need to learn the best way to deal with the school.

TALKING TO TEACHERS

One major thing has changed since you were at school - you've grown up! And that means you now have an entirely different relationship with the staff. Unfortunately, this doesn't always mean that it's any less scary. Teachers can be intimidating.

This isn't helped by the differences between nurseries and schools. For one thing, you - and your child - may have called the nursery staff by their first names, and found them more approachable. For another, teachers have more children in a class and are usually less able to chat. All this means that both teacher and school can seem less friendly than a cosy nursery setting.

But it doesn't mean the teachers actually *are* less friendly. The staff in the Reception classes, at least, tend to be warm and on the friendly side – but they do have a lot of children in a class and can sometimes be distracted when you try to talk to them. They can also seem a little stand-offish.

All teachers are trying to do their job, and we are (at least most of the time) on the same side, that of the children. We all want the best for them. Many teachers are also parents, so they can see issues from both sides. However, that doesn't mean the relationship between parents and teachers is friction-free.

If I'm honest, I don't think that teachers realise how daunting parents can find them. They'll be getting the room ready in the morning and the little ones (and you) will be waiting outside. The children, excited about the beginning of the day, may wave at the window, but the teachers often just ignore them. Why? I don't know!

> "Parents feel nervous about approaching a teacher. But teachers feel nervous too, about what parents think of them. It's a real shame that neither says 'I know how you feel.'"
> Julia Skinner, ex-primary school headteacher

Dealing with teachers is a tricky issue because there is so much scope for misunderstanding. A teacher who isn't that good with parents might be great with the children. This is often very true of new teachers, who need time to get more confident when dealing with all the mums and dads.

The best advice I can give you for getting on with your child's teachers is to be nice! Don't patronise them or be rude to them. Be polite, behave impeccably and hopefully they will do the same. Oh, and remember that they really appreciate a word of thanks every so often.

> “I would recommend that parents are polite, that they don't over-step the mark and that they don't bad-mouth the school as this invariably gets back to the teachers. Be aware that we're the professionals and that we want your child to be happy because happy children thrive and then do well academically. It needs to be a combined effort, with the parent, the child and the school.
>
> Jo Ebner, Headmistress of the Royal School, Hampstead, London”

The concept of “parents as partners” is one which was given a huge emphasis by the last Government. In other words, schools are supposed to work with parents, and so listen to your views. This means that they should (yes, I did say “should”!) be good at communication.

I have a problem: when should I speak to the teacher about it?

This is a very good question, and one which has a double answer. First, you should definitely speak to the teacher if you are worried or have something important to say. Don't be too scared.

> “If you're concerned, tell us. If we think there's an issue, we will start passing it along, from the teacher to the deputy head and then the head. If you think that the teacher hasn't done anything about an issue which is bothering you, you should go to the head anyway.
>
> Louise Robinson, Headmistress of Merchant Taylors' Girls' School, Crosby”

In terms of when to raise your concern, try not to do so first thing in the morning.

> “Morning is a very stressful time for a lot of teachers. They have to set up the classroom, perhaps have a morning meeting and welcome 30 kids. That means it's a difficult time to have a conversation with a parent.
> Tanja Perez-Williams, Reception class teacher”

This might seem obvious to you, but it had never crossed my mind there was anything wrong with catching the teacher at the beginning of the day. The response from teachers was unanimous: don't collar them when all the children are arriving. The exception to the rule is if it's about something very quick and relevant to the day ahead (for example, if your child is very tired because he had a late night).

It's also not wise to rant at a teacher in front of your child. You don't want to raise a question mark in his mind that there is an issue between teacher and parent. Instead, arrange a convenient time to speak.

Most teachers prefer it if you speak to them at the end of the day. This may, of course, not be possible, especially if you work and don't do the school pick-up. However, times are changing and a number of schools are happy for you to email the school office, or the teacher directly, to arrange a time which suits you both.

> “It's always better to sit down and have a conversation at a sensible time when neither of you is stressed. I use emails all the time, and many schools do that now, but you can also book a time for a telephone conversation.

That often suits working parents and can work really well.
Jo Ebner, Headmistress of the Royal School, Hampstead, London ”

Always tell the school if there is something which is going to affect your child. Things which happen at home (a new baby, you and your husband having problems) often affect a child at school, either with their learning, behaviour, or both.

What if there is a problem with the teacher herself?

If you feel unhappy about your child's teacher, don't let it fester. Talk to her directly, and then see if you need to take it further.

Your child will probably let you know if there's a problem at school, and sometimes (thankfully not too often) this is due to the teacher. It may be that she shouts a lot or, more worryingly, that your child says she "picks" on him. What you need to do is find out whether these complaints are true, and, rather than going in all guns blazing, attempt to deal with them. The impression you need to give is that you want to help – not that you're looking for someone's head on a platter!

“ You could suggest to the teacher that your child is struggling to form a relationship with him or her. Ask if she could try to keep an eye on what's going on and ask for suggestions on how best to work it out. Don't infer that it's the teacher's fault or accuse them. You need to be polite, but also need to get to the bottom of it.

Suggest meeting again in a few weeks to see how things have improved. ”
Margaret Morrisey, Parents Out Loud

By the way, the "she's always shouting" complaint is not uncommon. With this one, it may be wise to have a chat with a few other parents to see if their children have mentioned it or whether yours is particularly sensitive. If it does seem to be a real problem, then you should raise it with the headteacher.

“ If there is an issue with a teacher, you've got to raise your concerns. With the best will in the world, we'll defend our staff, but it will still cause a flag to be raised. If we're told the same thing about a teacher three times by different parents, we know we've got a problem. ”
Louise Robinson, Headmistress of
Merchant Taylors' Girls' School, Crosby

Most complaints should be dealt with via the class teacher first. But make sure you do this in a constructive way. Don't blame the teacher without listening to what she has to say. And don't get personal. It's also vital to remember that your child sees things from his vantage point only. And although you love him and trust him, he may not always be right.

If your conversations with the teacher don't result in any improvement, and you think this is an important issue, then you should take the complaint further. Write down conversations you have had or particular issues that have affected your child. Then go to the headteacher and if that doesn't work, take your problem to the governors.

It's a legal requirement that schools must have a complaints policy, so feel free to ask for the one for your school. The complaints policy will lay out exactly how you should go about making your point (for example, going first to the teacher, then the headteacher, and then the governing body). If you can't resolve your issue informally, then you can make a formal (i.e. written) complaint to the chair of governors. Other (extreme) avenues would include contacting Ofsted, your MP or even the Secretary of State for Education.

Don't go and see the headteacher with a group of other parents, as it can make the head feel under attack. Most parents have different issues anyway, and it's far better for the headteacher to address these separately.

But I'm worried about how the school will view me if I complain

"You are your child's advocate so need to be pushy, but you also need to be aware that you must keep relations warm if the school is to genuinely try their best for them. There is a double pressure to be both likeable and bulldozer-like!

Kayla, mother of two boys, both with special needs"

Every parent worries that a complaint might be taken out on their child. All I can say is that it shouldn't be. Many parents also worry about being seen as "pushy", and this is something which does come up. We are often loath to question a teacher, but just because teachers have "seen it all before" doesn't mean they are right about every child. It is a hard balancing act, but if you do have a real problem, you owe it to your child to try and sort it out.

PARENTS' EVENINGS

Schools are encouraged to communicate well with parents, and let them know how their children are doing. One important way they do this is through parents' evenings.

Most schools have at least one, often two parents' evening a year. It's common for schools to hold a parents' evening in the first term (usually October or November) when the teacher is just getting to know your child. Some schools then hold another one at the beginning of the spring term, while others wait until the end of the academic year to follow up.

The early parents' evenings are designed to give us the opportunity to raise any specific issues, so don't be scared to do this. True, the situation can be a little daunting (those tiny chairs don't help), but if there is something you want to ask, now's the time to do it.

Parents disagree on the importance of parents' evenings. For many of us, they are little more than an opportunity to see the teacher without lots of other children about. And, if your child is happy and doing well, they can seem a bit like a waste of time. They are also often arranged at inconvenient times (4.30pm till 6pm, for example). If this affects you, think about asking the headteacher or governors if this can be changed and more evening appointments added.

If you don't have much to say, and it's the beginning of the school year, then your parents' evening may be brief. The teacher might say something vague (what a nice child you have, how well he is doing) and then ask you if you have anything you want to talk about. You probably won't.

But parents' evenings can be useful. So, if there is something which is bothering you, or if the teacher feels that she needs to discuss something important with you, be open to what she has to say.

> Parents evenings are about whether parents can handle the truth. Some parents just want affirmation that their child is bright and making progress. Sadly that's not always the case and parents don't always want to accept this reality.
>
> Hugh Greenwood, Headteacher of Boughton-under-Blean and Dunkirk Primary School

Parents' evenings often only allow around 10 minutes for each appointment, so do try to be punctual. If you have a specific concern which you want to discuss, it's probably wise to make an appointment at another time.

> "As a former deputy head and class teacher for 22 years I really think coming with an open mind, a notebook and some thoughtful questions is a really great way to arrive at parents' evening (while leaving your own experiences of school in the car park!). I really used to enjoy meeting all the parents; I felt parents' evening was a very important part of school life."
>
> Sue Atkins, parenting expert

Parents' evening checklist

1) Prepare questions

You may want to ask particular questions such as "is my child happy at school?" and "is he making friends?" Ask if the teacher has set any targets for your child (though this will become more relevant as they move up the school) and how you can help your child at home.

2) Talk to your child beforehand

Find out if he has anything he wants you to address.

3) Don't take the kids

As the children get older, some schools suggest bringing them with, but little ones will just distract you.

4) Don't just expect good feedback!

It can be really hard to hear that your child is not doing well, either socially or academically. But don't become defensive. Your child's teacher wants the best for him and needs to communicate any problems to you. Listen to these and ask what you can do to help.

“We had a rather disastrous parents evening when my son was in Reception. The teacher basically told us that our son was not really coping with the work, especially in maths. We were devastated – and very shocked. But when I look back now, I think it was a bit of a wake-up call. We started to help our son with his numbers, doing simple things like playing board games, and counting the number of steps we climbed when out, and we made an appointment to see the teacher again to see how it was going. He's now doing well, but it was still a surprise.
Alex, father of a daughter aged 8 and a son aged 6”

5) Don't criticise other teachers or parents

6) Follow up

Ask for another appointment if there are any problems or issues you need to discuss.

THE HOME-SCHOOL AGREEMENT

You will probably come across this very early on, and be asked to sign it. It's a document which lays out some of your responsibilities (making sure the children wear uniform, for example) and the school's (for example, that they will be welcoming and communicative). It's supposed to be put together by school, parents and pupils (although this isn't always the case) and may also include a section on what the school expects of its pupils.

Some home-school agreements can be very detailed and this can get parental backs up, particularly as parts relate to how children behave when they are at school (when we have no control over them). For example, they might be told to "show consideration to others at all times" or "always listen to others".

Clearly, these are not ridiculous suggestions, and most of us (all, I'd hope!) would like our children to behave well. However, I can understand why some parents might find signing a ticklist of how your 4-year-old should behave rather uninviting.

You should note that, as it says on the Government's own website "refusal to sign an agreement should not result in adverse consequences for a pupil or parent and cannot be made a condition of entry to the school". However, it might not give off the best impression when you are new to a school. In any case, free schools and academies are not held to this.

You can see more on home-school agreements on the Government's website, http://dfe.gov.uk/schools/pupilsupport/parents/a0014718/home-school-agreements

BEHAVIOUR AND DISCIPLINE

Although all state schools must have policies on behaviour and discipline (often called something more appealing like a "behaviour management policy"), they differ between schools.

The behaviour/discipline and complaints policies may be on the school's website, or given out with other information when your child starts school. However, if your school is not very good at providing information, just ask for a copy. It's much better to know what's expected.

> “First time school parents can find it hard getting their heads round discipline issues which can be complex. They can go through the roof the first time their child is disciplined! That's why I think it's really important to familiarise yourself with the discipline policy. Don't be scared to ask what the rules and systems are.”
>
> Garry, father of two boys

The policies usually talk about promoting “positive behaviour” and ensuring that behaviour leads to better learning. Children will be told about how they should behave in school, and should know the consequences if they don't behave well. Encouraging positive behaviour may take the form of a “star of the week” book or sticker, or golden time (where the whole class gets some special time to do what they want because all have behaved well). Individual teachers may also have their own reward schemes (sticker charts, for example).

Don't assume that your child will behave in exactly the same way at school as he does at home.

Many a parent has been astonished by a messy child who can't seem to follow rules at home, but is praised for his helpfulness at school. Sadly, many others have been surprised by quite the opposite. You need to listen to the teacher on this.

> “You shouldn't always believe your own child, especially if the school has flagged up a problem. They wouldn't call you in unless there was an issue. Think about it, why would they?”
>
> Jo Ebner, Headmistress of the Royal School, Hampstead, London

Ways of dealing with bad behaviour may range from a child being moved away from a friend in the classroom, to having his privileges withdrawn (not having playtime for example). There may be a traffic-light system (tell your children to stay on green!), or different coloured bands (a child may need a band to go inside at lunchtime). These rules can be complicated for young children, so it's worth familiarising yourself with them in order to help explain them.

GETTING INVOLVED

Schools need volunteers, but it's up to you how much - or little - you want to get involved. Sometimes this involvement takes place on an ad hoc basis. You might offer to come along on a school trip, for example, man the class stall for half an hour at the fête or come in regularly and hear the little ones read. Or you may decide to make a bigger commitment.

There are three main, official, ways to contribute to the life of the school; via the parent teacher association (the PTA or PA), the governing body or the parents' council. You're most likely to come across the PTA first.

The PTA

Some PTAs have very close links between parents and teachers. Others have dropped the "T" from the name, and are simply concerned parents. Most have at least one teacher attending meetings and all of them help out at school.

PTAs usually do wonders for schools, mainly through fundraising or organising events such as Christmas or summer fairs. But this doesn't mean that they are universally loved. In some schools, they may have a hard time with staff, who can be suspicious of their motives and enthusiasm. At others, parents themselves may find some PTA members to be over-the-top and cliquey.

“ Schools are surrounded by a coterie of self-serving, cliquey 'saints' who expect thanks for doing stuff which adds nothing to kids' education and which eats up time and family life and adds to our collective guilt about child raising. Now, that's the real truth of it, isn't it?”

Justine

“I don't volunteer for the PTA because I am a 'saint' nor do I do it out of guilt. I do it because personally I feel the need to contribute to the community in which my family live. If you want to sneer at that, go ahead. I don't see it as a competition. I just think it's good for the whole school.”

Lydia, mother of two, aged 9 and 3

If you're new to a school, then the PTA might be something that you will find extremely useful. It's true that not everyone is the kind of person who loves to organise events, but if you join up, you will meet new people.

“I got involved in my first year at school, when I didn't really know anybody. Joining the PTA meant that I met parents across the school. It's for the kids, but I'd say that it helped me to make friends too.”

Haruko, mother of two daughters, aged 6 and 4

It shouldn't be too difficult to find out about your PTA. Their details will probably be on your school's website, or on any information booklets that you've been sent. If you can't find out who to contact, simply ask the school office. Many schools have PTA representatives in each class.

Bringing up children and trying to do everything else in your life isn't always easy. Sometimes it's easy to sound negative about things which are supposed to be enjoyable, and help others. The PTA is one of these areas.

So, be warned (and the PTA at my children's school won't thank me for pointing this out), there is always a shortage of volunteers. This means that if you do offer to help at an event, the chances are that you will be asked again. There is a real hunger for more people to get involved, but sometimes you have to say no. Personally I think that you should help out when you can, but you also need to make sure that school events don't take over your life. A good school needs committed parent helpers to make a strong community, but sometimes it can be hard to get people to agree to help out.

> “Sometimes you feel as if you're putting in so much time and effort, and that no one else is. That's dangerous as you can get resentful – and I did. I chaired our PTA for a year and tried so hard to make it all work. But people only got in touch to complain. They saw it as a place to come and moan. That's not to say that the PTA isn't important. I really think it is. It's a way to support the school, and to build on the community there.
>
> Carrie, mum of 3

Some PTA roles – chairperson or treasurer for example –are an awful lot of work. Don't take these on unless you have the time, and you know you aren't going to regret it.

Not every school has a PTA. If you're interested in setting one up, you could contact the NCPTA (National Confederation of Parent Teacher Associations) at www.ncpta.org.uk.

> I'd say the PTA is fun, the governors is the serious stuff, and the School Council can be both!
>
> "Ptamum"

Should you become a governor?

Governors are an indispensable part of any school, but it's often difficult for the average parent (that's you and me) to understand what they are, not to mention what they do. The problem is that the governors of the school often make up an extra clique, with an air of self-important mystique about them. After all, they understand the inner-workings of the school and you don't. And sometimes they really make you know it.

But not all governors are like this, and many are there because they really want to help. They are open to your complaints and suggestions and want to change things. The problem is, they always seem to be a little stressed about it.

> Being a governor gives you a very valuable insight into how the school operates. I was asked to do it and agreed for the good of the school and my children's education. I feel I did it for all the right reasons, but I knew it was potentially lots of work and went in knowing I would have a constant guilt trip. There's just so much to do and you can't do it all.
>
> Jackie, mother of three, aged 9, 7 and 4

If you've just joined a school and you're the kind of person who a) likes to get involved or b) wants to change things (already? That's quick), then becoming a governor might be for you. But you need to make a distinction between being involved in the education of your child and being involved in the running of the school.

Some people fancy becoming a parent governor because they're a bit nosey about what's going on in the school, and/or because they think it will help their child. Both these desires may fade quickly into the background once you realise how much there is to do. I know someone who stood for a governor position because (I'm not being unfair here) she was on something of a power trip and wanted to show other parents how fabulous she was. She then couldn't handle the extra work and resigned after six months.

Every school has a governing body which has a number of important statutory duties (more on this below) and makes key decisions in the running of the school. In most schools about a third of the governors are parent governors. There will also be some staff governors (not more than one third), someone from the local authority, the community and (depending on the type of school), representatives from the foundation or partnership which set it up. All state schools are accountable to their governing bodies, and in turn, the governing bodies are accountable to parents and the local community (not that most of us really understand what that means).

> "You get out what you put in and you really have to devote time to it. If you've got the time and are interested, I would recommend it, because the strategic running of a school is relevant to us all – whether for our children, or for the greater good of the community."
>
> Garry, father of two boys

As Garry says, the governors are seen as a "strategic body", and the idea is that they set the purposes and aims of the school, among other things. For example, they get involved in the staffing structure, pay policy and appointment of the headteacher and deputy headteacher (yes, they're to blame if the leadership team is poor). They are also responsible for the admission policy, pupil behaviour and monitoring, as well as approving the budget. Some people describe the governors as being a "critical friend to the school" and it's obvious that they work very closely with the headteacher, who reports to them on all sorts of issues. The general rule is that governors should carry out between 10 to 20 full-time days a year in their roles, plus ad hoc committee meetings. They are also encouraged to take training courses. And all this is voluntary!

It's all very official, with meetings "serviced" by a clerk and headed by a chair and vice-chair. Each governing body has different committees such as personnel, curriculum, finance and ICT, and these have their own meetings too.

You can't just become a parent governor; you have to wait for a slot to become available. Then you can stand for election. Other parents will have to nominate you and you may find yourself up against a number of your fellow mums and dads. There will then be a vote.

Most schools allow those who are standing to write something noble about themselves on a pamphlet which is then circulated before votes are cast. But to be honest, people usually vote for people they know.

As a new parent you are at something of a disadvantage here. Parents with children in different year groups will know more people. In other words, it is something of a popularity contest.

This may sound unnerving. None of us like to lose a vote, and I'm sure this has stopped many people from standing in the past. However, at some schools people have to be really cajoled into standing – and it's not hard to be elected if you have no competition.

Being a governor can be extremely rewarding, teaching you a great deal about your child's school, and in particular what goes on behind the scenes. It also allows you, as a parent, to have an input, and to directly influence the vision and strategy of the school.

“ Some people go in without realising what a governor actually is. They think it's a bit like the PTA or just being a cheerleader for the school but with slightly more power. However, it's different from the PTA. It's a strategic role; governors must challenge the headteacher as well as support the school.

Emma Knights, chief executive of the National Governors' Association ”

Personally, I find it interesting how many men choose to volunteer for being a governor, but won't get involved with the PTA. I wonder if this might be down to governors having more power – and men therefore thinking it's more worthy of their time. Explaining this disparity to me, one (male) governor told me, "Well, I'm not really a tombola type of person!"

“ I sometimes think that being a governor was a step too far for me. There are so many meetings and many of them are utterly tedious. Being on the PTA was much more rewarding because I could find a job which suited my skills, but I know that some people look down on the PTA. No one does that with the governors!

Stephanie, mother of two and parent governor ”

For more on governors, visit the National Governors' Association, www.nga.org.uk.

The NGA publish an induction booklet for new governors: www.nga.org.uk/guidesmain.aspx.

Note: private schools, which are set up as charitable organisations, also have governors, but a different type of governing body. They don't have elections for parent governors in the same way as state schools, and although parents are able to get involved as governors, their job is not to be a parental representative in any way.

Parent councils

Just in case you think that schools don't have enough organisations, they are also encouraged to set up parent councils (or forums). The idea behind these is to discuss what's going on in the school and give parents a "voice". In a way, they do fill a gap between the PTA and the governors, but I'm not sure all schools have enough parents to go round!

You can find out more about parent councils via the Parent Councils UK website, www.parentcouncils.co.uk.

> "Parent councils are a good option in order to get a real voice of parents, across the board. Parent governors don't actually represent parents – it's not their job to do that. But the governing body needs to understand what parents think. It is important that the school has a way of listening to all views. Parent councils give people the opportunity for more involvement and an increased understanding of how the school works.
>
> Emma Knights, chief executive of the National Governors' Association"

Many schools also have school councils for the *pupils* in their schools. Each year (possibly from Year 2 or 3 upwards) has council representatives to represent their views.

Volunteering

Schools love parents to help out, but these days, many schools won't let you do so unless you have had a Criminal Records Bureau (CRB) or

Disclosure Scotland check. Not all schools insist on this as it does depend what the volunteering activity is. It's wise to ask the school about their policy. The check usually takes around four to six weeks, so if you know it's something the school insists on, try to get ahead with it. Often, they will sort out the paperwork and apply on your behalf.

> "If I'd known about the CRB check as soon as Danny started school, I'd have made sure I got one much earlier. Not having one meant that I couldn't join him on his trip to Butterfly World. Mind you, perhaps it's good that mummy didn't go on his first ever trip with the school!"
>
> Joanna, mother of Danny, aged 5

Children usually love it when their parents volunteer, so, if you can, try to help out every so often (but don't beat yourself up about it if this proves impossible).

Regular helpers (for example, those who read with children once or twice a week) may be asked to sign an agreement or verbally agree not to "disclose" what goes on while they're in the classroom. I think this is patronising, and just another demonstration of how some schools panic about parents knowing "too much". However, if you're asked to sign it, you probably should.

Volunteering to help out on school trips is actually a bit of a sore point for me, as I have applied to go on every one since my daughter started school, but have never been lucky enough to be "picked out of the hat". This year I actually asked the teacher if I was blacklisted! She laughed and said that they genuinely do it randomly. I just hope I'm not thought of as the kind of parent described by this anonymous teacher.

> "Ah, the class trips and the headache they cause for all teachers. After years of trips and parents coming in to help, I've had:

- parents who shout/talk to the children as they would their own (not in a positive way)
- a parent who 'needed' ciggie breaks (I kid you not!)
- a parent who wanted their child in their group but whose child did not want this at all.
- parents who report back to the playground mums about the attitude/behaviour of particular children (I was furious!)
- a parent who helped out at netball match and turned up to offer lifts. . .drunk. ”

"Anonymous"

In some schools, it can be a struggle getting enough parents to volunteer, so you might be lucky and go on lots of trips. They are often particularly keen on dads volunteering, as they can then take groups of boys to the loo!

Paying for trips

School trips are rarely free, even if the cost is just to cover transport. The school will probably ask you to make a "voluntary contribution" towards your child's outing and, if you can afford this, it's obviously wise to do so (otherwise the school will end up meeting the cost out of its budget or cancelling because they can't cover the costs). However, the school is not allowed to *force* you to pay, and if you feel that you can't afford it, you should raise this with the class teacher or headteacher. Your child cannot legally be left out of a school trip because his parents haven't paid for him to go.

TEACHING ASSISTANTS

Teaching assistants (also described as TAs) are part of what are known as "learning support staff" at a school and probably weren't about in your day. Every Reception class has a TA, but it will depend on the school as to whether they have them in every year. Your child's TA may be known by a different title - for example, a classroom or learning assistant.

The role of a TA varies from school to school and some have a specialism such as literacy or numeracy. All work under the guidance of the class teacher, but within this they may work with the whole class, a small group, or even a particular child. Unless they are a HLTA (higher level teaching assistant), they won't take over teaching an entire class if the teacher is off work.

With the little ones, the TA's role is usually to be a support to the teacher (perhaps helping to prepare the classroom for lessons, or reading with a small group) and a warm, wonderful support to the kids too. It's definitely worth getting to know yours. All TAs I've met have been terrific.

The TA is often the person who knows what's really going on between children. This may be because they are usually on playground duty or possibly because they're the ones who cheer up children who are sad or who have had an accident!

WORKING PARENTS, SCHOOL HOURS AND AFTER-SCHOOL CLUBS

"School hours are very different from childminder hours and it's so stressful and complex when your child starts school. I've found it really hard to

> manage working hours, childminders and after-school clubs.
>
> Helen

Being a working parent and having children at school is a balancing act. Although it's a sign that your child is growing up, it creates new problems. If you've had a nanny, is it really affordable to keep her on for after-school and holidays? Will the childminder do the school pick-up, or can you find childcare to cover after-school hours until 6.30pm?

This is when parents need to be a bit creative! Can you swap childcare with other mums – hosting regular playdates on specific days? Can your parents or in-laws help out, or is there a local sixth-former or granny who might be interested in working for three hours a few days a week? Ask other parents for suggestions on how to find good childcare, or if they are interested in sharing care.

> Childcare got more difficult when my daughter started school. She had been at a full-time nursery, but now we had to work out after-school care, especially as my husband and I both work full time. The only way I could see to deal with it was by getting an au pair. But that created its own issues!
>
> Jennifer Howze, mother of a daughter aged 7 and stepson, aged 12

I have, at different times, successfully found people through word of mouth, putting a card up in a local bookshop and via websites such as Netmums. Putting up small advertisements locally – the library or doctor's surgery, for example – is a good idea. However, make sure you get references personally.

All parents of young children now have the right to request flexible working hours (if they have been employed by a company for at least

26 weeks by the time they make their request). If this is something you want to do, you need to speak to your employer. It may be that you ask to work from home on certain days, or have more free time during the holidays.

> "The key is to have a straightforward conversation with your employer, and find out what will fit for you and for the business. Employers are increasingly seeing the business benefits of helping support their employees: they can retain people for longer and they have employees with a better work-life balance.
>
> Ben Willmott, The Chartered Institute of Personnel Development"

Of course, this may sound like cloud cuckooland to some of you. It may be that changing hours is impossible, and that having a child who finishes school at any time from 3pm onwards is a real problem. Coping with it can be very stressful.

> "Working parents need to:
>
> - accept that it's hard and that you will always feel you're neglecting one or the other
> - be firm at work and leave on time, otherwise it will start slipping and work will take over
> - always pay for your childcare on time and work out a reasonable cancellation policy for both carer and parent. Find out what these are, for example, if you need to cancel after-school club a week in advance or forfeit payment

- treat childcare cover on business terms. This saves friends and family for emergency cover. Remember, if you rely on friends for childcare then you may find yourself spending a lot of time returning favours
- don't feel guilty if other mums help out in class or go on school trips. Do what you can, when you can, so that your child sees you're involved somehow at school
- try to 'put work away', mentally and physically, when the kids are around. They can tell if you're preoccupied. (I wish I could listen to this bit of advice – it's my major failing as a mum.) ”

Eleanor, mother of two sons, aged 7 and 4

Other than the (not small) problem of childcare, being a working parent (or indeed any parent with other commitments) can also be problematic when it comes to school events. Sometimes it seems as if schools don't take this into account at all.

“ As a working mother I am frequently annoyed and let down by the school's attitude that parents can drop everything at a moment's notice. I am supposed to give six weeks' notice for ANY leave, so when the school sends letters home with less than two weeks' notice it makes it very difficult. ”

Sally, mother of one son, aged 6

Some schools have taken this on board, and send out dates as soon as they can. One headteacher told me that she would do almost anything but change these once they have gone out. She realises that it's not fair to the parents. Others are less helpful, not only with days, but also timings. They don't seem to realise that putting on an event at 10.30am means a whole morning off.

If you want change in your school, you should contact the PTA or parent governors before going to the headteacher. It may be an issue which has been raised before, but that's no reason why it can't change. I certainly believe that school events should be arranged at the beginning or end of the day.

> “Schools have so many events that it can be difficult to go them all. If you have a partner, try to share them out, or ask grandparents or aunts and uncles. The children don't mind who is there, as long as someone's turned up for them!”
>
> Haruko, mother of two daughters, aged 6 and 4

After-school clubs

Many schools now offer breakfast and after-school clubs to help with childcare. These can range in price, depending on whether they are specific clubs (ballet or karate for example) or are there to help out working parents by opening early (often from 7.30am) and closing at around 6pm.

After-school clubs really vary in quality. Ask around at your school to see what reputation they have. Breakfast and after-school clubs are often very over-subscribed so find out if you have to have to book in advance.

> “A good after-school club offers a variety of activities that enables children to develop new skills, build confidence and make new friends. My daughter

attends her school's after-school club once a week. Admittedly, I use it for childcare but it's a really well organised club that offers a variety of activities, including cookery, art and sewing. ”
Natasha, mother of a daughter, aged 5

After-school clubs tend to be good value (around £2.50 or £3 a session) and an easy, convenient way for your kids to be looked after, but they are very different to more personalised childcare like childminders or nannies. It's more about looking after lots of children at once and can seem a bit impersonal, at least at the beginning.

“ Don't expect the after-school club to do much more than you would after school. Essentially you're paying for warmth and safety. Kids need downtime, a snack and the chance to play. Accept they'll watch TV or video games and that you're paying for the privilege! ”
Eleanor, mother of two sons, aged 7 and 4

Some after-school clubs cater for several different schools. Make sure you check where your club is based, and if not, how the children get there. Do they walk or go in a minibus? If the club is for children from different schools, make sure you explain this to your child, so they won't be thrown by mixing with children they don't know.

School life is complicated and we haven't actually tackled one important thing yet. . .ah yes, learning.

8

Actual learning

When your child starts school (and perhaps before) you and he are introduced to a world of edu-speak. This is particularly true for explanations of the curriculum, so you are sure to hear much talk of a "play-based" curriculum, of National Curriculum "stages" and of your child's "learning goals". But take heart, I'm going to cut through the jargon.

THE CONCEPT

The Reception year is part of the Early Years Foundation Stage (sometimes known by its initials, EYFS), which was introduced in September 2008, and actually covers "learning, development and care" from birth to age 5. So if your child has already been to nursery or with a child-minder, he will have been following this curriculum there too.

My son followed the EYFS in his Reception class last year and I have to say that I was really impressed. To put it simply, he had fun *and* he learnt.

This is precisely the idea behind the curriculum for Reception-aged children – that they learn through play. They sit much less than we used to (you won't see any desks in your child's classroom). Instead they explore and do, and there is a lot of freedom to play either in or out of the classroom. The atmosphere is relaxed and the day is less structured than you might expect.

The idea behind learning through play is that your child does something enjoyable (pours cups of water into a large jug, for example) but at the same time, learns (about capacity in this instance). He will often be able to choose what he wants to do, taking the resources he needs.

Children in the UK start school at a young age (4 or 5) as opposed to 6, for example, in France and Germany, and 7 in Finland and Sweden. This is not the forum for a discussion about the benefits or disadvantages of such a young starting age. However, the EYFS has been designed to take age into account.

> "We have huge expectations on our very young children, but you've got to remember how little they are. I think it's fantastic that children now have this more nurturing, play-based way to learn."
> Tanja Perez-Williams, Reception class teacher

But despite all this emphasis on play, and the stress on every child being an individual, learning at school can set off a whole new strand of competitive behaviour. And as you may have guessed, this is usually between parents, not children. You need to try very hard not to get caught up in this. Remember, other children (as long as they are not upsetting yours) are almost irrelevant!

Note: Despite the optimism shown above, there are people who are unhappy about the EYFS curriculum because it involves "targets" for young children. Personally I don't think the targets are unrealistic, nor that there is any evidence that undue pressure is being put on children to achieve them. There is no formal testing, just constant observation on the part of the teacher.

However, things may soon change. The new Coalition Government is currently carrying out a(nother) review of the curriculum and the Education Secretary, Michael Gove, recently announced that he is thinking of publishing school-by-school results for the Early Years stage. This may put an extra pressure onto schools and teachers.

THE CLASSROOM

The classroom itself will look very different from your day - not least because of the more welcoming layout! The children often sit on a big carpet for group activities (yours will probably soon start talking about his "carpet space") and there'll be no blackboard. Instead, each classroom usually has an interactive whiteboard connected up to a computer.

The classroom will look more like a place to play than a school, with dressing up clothes, construction toys, books and jigsaws. In fact, it will probably look a lot like your child's pre-school.

If it's a school with more than one class in each year, then children may be able to go freely from room to room and there might be a shared meeting space in the middle too.

WHAT DO THEY LEARN?

All schools in England follow the same National Curriculum for this age-group and the EYFS is split into six areas of "learning and development".

The idea is that your child will achieve certain "early learning goals" (the infamous "targets") in each of these areas by the end of Reception. Of course, some children will go beyond these (this can be a problem, if the teacher doesn't seem interested in extending them much beyond the box that has now been ticked), while others won't manage them. Most of the headings are broken down into further sub-headings, as you can see from the government-issued reference sheet found here: www.qcda.gov.uk/resources/assets/poster_v8_aw.pdf.

If the six areas aren't already familiar, they soon will be! If your school sends home a newsletter each week, they will probably explain what the children have been up to, using these headings. As you will soon learn, the curriculum is very prescriptive.

The headings and subcategories are as follows.

1) Communication, language and literacy (which is broken down further into)
   - language for communication and thinking
   - linking sounds and letters
   - reading
   - writing
2) Personal, social and emotional development (which is broken down further into)
   - dispositions and attitudes
   - social development
   - emotional development
3) Problem solving, reasoning and numeracy (which is broken down further into)
   - numbers as labels and for counting
   - calculating
   - shape, space and measures
4) Knowledge and understanding of the world
5) Creative development
6) Physical development

Your school may use different names, for example "mathematics" for problem solving, reasoning and numeracy.

HOW DOES THE TEACHER TEACH?

When your child starts in Reception, his teacher will carry out a "Foundation Stage profile" to see what he knows already, and how his learning can be developed over the year. This profile is very informal and is really for your teacher's benefit.

Teachers assess children, informally, throughout the year. They make constant observations of what they are doing and add these to the profile. That way it's easy to see how a child progresses.

The teacher will usually make a folder of your child's work which you should be able to look at whenever you like and keep at the end of the year.

At the end of Reception, the teacher will complete an EYFS profile which assesses how your child has done against all the "early learning goals". Each heading has a nine-point scale (lowest = 1, highest = 9). It sounds complicated, and it is. It also takes an awful lot of time to do. . .Teachers sometimes need our sympathy!

At the end of the year you will be given a summary of this profile (which will make up your child's school report). You can ask for the complete profile if you like. A teacher should flag up any concerns, but if your child is only getting scores of between 1 and 3 on any of the levels, you should take note, speak to the teacher and see how you can help.

Age can really make a difference when your child starts school, in both his behaviour, and ability to learn. Some children are almost a year older than others (those with September birthdays as opposed to those with August birthdays). Take this into account before starting to panic, and remember that when it comes to Reception, social development is as important as learning.

Differentiation

After a short time at school, you may notice that the children are sometimes put into ability groups as well as taught within the whole class. You might find this out by the class newsletter, which will, apparently innocuously, mention the fact that "some children" learnt certain letters one week or counted beyond 20. Let's be honest, this does make sense and the idea is that teachers can switch things around depending on different children's needs and abilities.

If some children are advanced in numeracy and/or literacy, it's sensible for them to move a little faster. It does not mean that they will be going to Oxbridge (although they might). Nor does it mean that the children who find learning to read or count that bit harder will never catch up (they will). It's all done for the benefit of the child.

In addition, children are usually put into mixed-ability groups/tables which are called something that doesn't suggest any one of them is more important than any other (red or blue, apples or bananas).

SO, WHAT DO THEY DO?

Each of the six headings contains information on a huge list of topics. The most controversial is Communication, Language and Literacy, in other words, reading and writing. Your child will spend an awful lot of school time on this topic as this is emphasised in the National Curriculum.

COMMUNICATION, LANGUAGE AND LITERACY

There has been much recent hand-wringing about British children's capabilities in literacy. One thing which has been particularly flagged up is the importance of communication, of children becoming competent not just in reading and writing, but speaking and listening. This really is important. As I mentioned in chapter 2, simply having a two-way conversation with your child sets him off on the right footing.

While in Reception, children will be encouraged to listen and also talk about their own experiences. They will role-play and make up their own stories. They will also learn the beginnings of reading and writing.

The crucial idea of learning through play takes place in a number of different ways. You may find that your child goes on "listening walks" around the school, noting down the different sounds he hears, or that he plays games, becoming a detective who solves letter clues.

The classroom is often used creatively, setting up a café (children can give and take down orders and count out money), nursery (they can teach babies about letters and numbers), or travel agent (lots of scope for making tickets). Often the teachers follow the child's lead on this (for example, a child who loved cars might want to open a garage).

Reading

Obviously children enter school with different early reading experiences. Some recognise their names but don't know the alphabet, others are already reading. The teacher will try to differentiate work depending on a child's ability, but it takes time to assess a whole class. So, if you feel your child is on the wrong "reading book" early on, wait a few weeks before mentioning it. However, if this continues, you should raise the issue.

Reading is one of the few areas in which comparisons can be made easily between young children. That may explain why it's something of an incendiary issue for parents! Many have been known to sneak a look at the reading book brought by another child on a playdate. Why? Either to pat yourself (and implicitly your child) on the back for his ability or to bemoan the fact that he is behind. It's a strange kind of parental torture. . .

But while learning to read is not a competition, it's certainly true that it can be painful trying to work out what the different levels of reading books mean, and whether your child is on the right one.

In order to help your child learn to read, he will soon be put onto a Reading Scheme. The most common is the Oxford Reading Tree series, which features a family with very odd names (no Janet and John here; instead we have Biff and Kipper). Like all the other reading schemes, the books get harder as your child progresses. And some children progress far more quickly than others.

However, you should remember that the aim is for your child to learn to read, and to love reading. Reading opens up so many other avenues in life, so you don't want to put on too much pressure or make reading feel like a chore. It's not a race.

Children will probably start bringing reading books home by the first half-term, although some schools send them home earlier, and others may wait until after Christmas. The book (it might be one or more a week) will usually come with a "reading record" book for you to write a comment in.

Reading rants

You're not alone if you find the first reading books a bit tedious, especially if you are supposed to read them through a few times.

Wordless books

Your child may come home with a book containing no words, only pictures. This can create problems as many 4-year-olds, now delighted at being in school, see such books as "babyish". It's also confusing for parents – how does a book with no words help a child to learn to read?

> "I was amazed when my daughter brought home a short book with pictures and no words. I really had no idea what to do. We looked at it and guessed what the story might be, but that took all of 30 seconds. I didn't really get it."
>
> "Noidea"

Wordless books are about comprehension rather than reading ability. Your child's teacher does not want him to learn to read without understanding *what* he is reading, so these books offer the opportunity to take an interest in the story itself and what he thinks might be happening. In some schools they call these "story walks", where a child develops his story-telling skills.

You are supposed to ask your child questions about the book, so he can show you how well he understands the story. Your child's teacher should tell you this – it's her mistake if she hasn't mentioned the rationale behind the book – and you may want to follow this up (politely of course) by asking for any tips on how to "read" these kinds of books.

> Teaching a child to read is not all about reading the words and sounds. It's about enjoying a book, being imaginative and understanding it. We often send home ideas for questions you could ask with reading books – for example, what's happening in the picture, or what do you think happens next?
>
> Tanja Perez-Williams, Reception class teacher

Being on the wrong book level

However laid back a parent you are, you may, at some stage, find yourself caught up in whether your child is on the right reading level for his ability. This can become a real issue if your child was reading before he went to school.

As a general rule, your child is on the right book level if he is getting around nine out of 10 words right.

> My youngest daughter has always been good at reading, but when she started school, she was put on a level of reading book which was far too easy for her. I could see she was becoming switched off from reading. I even felt she was going backwards! I spoke to the teacher who moved her up one level. It made no difference. Eventually I spoke to the teacher again. I think that's when she took notice. Grace moved up four levels and was finally being challenged.

> I hated looking pushy, but there didn't seem to be anything else I could do. ”
> Simone, mother of three girls

Simone did the right thing. This is really common and you could always start with a (courteous) note in the reading book saying that you don't think your child has been assessed at the correct level. If nothing changes, speak to the teacher, but don't be aggressive. Instead ask why your child is on a particular level AND mention that you think it might not be the right one. It may be (as mentioned in the wordless books) that your child can read the words properly, but that he doesn't actually understand the story. (See pp. 129–131 on speaking to teachers in the right way).

Teachers are always assessing your child and his ability, so they should be able to spot if he is on the right level. Of course, the books may also be too difficult for your child, and this is something to address as well. You don't want him to give up. Whatever happens, keep reading, even if it's just you to him for a while.

As you will soon spot, your child's school book will probably be quite different from a "normal" book. So, if you can, keep reading other books, either from your own collection or from a library. Children can easily become familiar with the layout of their reading scheme books and it's really useful if they also look at other texts from an early age. By texts, I mean anything in written form - comics, catalogues or books. Many boys enjoy non-fiction and love big books like *The Guinness Book of Records*. In addition, your school may allow them to have a "free choice" book each week too.

If you want to continue reading scheme type books, there are lots of these about. Try the Rigby Star series, Songbirds Phonics, Collins Big Cat, Dancing Bear or the new Floppy and Friends phonics books from the Oxford Reading Tree, www.oup.com/oxed/primary/oxfordreadingtree. Jolly Phonics, www.jollylearning.co.uk, and Read Write Inc., www.oup.com/oxed/primary/rwi, also sell their own books. You could also take a look at Reading Chest, www.readingchest.co.uk, which is a rental service for reading scheme books.

What do I write in the reading diary?

The reading diary is a forum for communication between teacher and parent, it's not just there to praise your child (or criticise his teacher). So, I'd recommend being honest in the book, saying something like "He read this well, but struggled with these words".

However, the reading diary might not always be checked every day, so if you have any major concerns, speak to the teacher directly.

No child can learn to read without help and support. Although it may seem like a chore, it's really important that you help your child with his reading. He needs to practise. It's particularly good if dads get involved, so little boys don't think that reading is just something girls do.

"Motivation is a key issue when getting children to learn to read. I sit with mine each day and they read to me or their dad. It breaks my heart when I see some parents who just can't be bothered to help their children read. It is a lovely time of day when everyone is relaxed and we can read together."
Emma, mother of two girls, aged 5 and 7

All schools send home reading books, but some will add other "homework" in the form of words to learn or particular letters to trace round too.

How does my child learn to read?

This is the other major issue connected with reading - how they learn to do it.

Synthetic phonics

It comes as a shock when you are thrown back into the education system, this time as a parent instead of a pupil. Our children learn differently these days, not just because of technology, but because teaching methods have changed. Schools now do their maths by partitioning, using numberbonds and numberlines (more on p. 172) and teach children to read via synthetic phonics.

Phonics, of course, is not new, but it went out of favour some time ago. Now it is back, recommended highly by all political parties. The last Government introduced its own reading scheme ("Letters and Sounds", which may be what your child is following, www.letters-and-sounds.com), while the current Conservative/Lib. Dem. coalition has made its fondness for phonics very clear. In fact, the Government is planning a reading test for 6-year-olds – along synthetic phonics lines.

When my daughter started in Reception, I was baffled by this. I soon realised that she was saying letter sounds instead of the names of letters (sssss instead of "ess" for S), but that was about as far as my understanding went. Yet in a nutshell, that is exactly what synthetic phonics is about. It's all to do with using the pure sounds created by each letter, then blending them to create words. It's based on the 44 sounds (called phonemes, the smallest units of sound) which make up English (not just the 26 letters of the alphabet, but small groups of letters such as "sh" or "oo"), and gives children blocks of language to build on. This way they should be able to "decode" (or to put it simply, work out) words themselves.

You may have been taught to read in quite a different way, perhaps using flashcards and/or a kind of recognition method whereby you learnt whole words. A major problem here was that it meant children were not really being given the tools to decode new words.

There are actually two kinds of phonics, analytic and synthetic. In analytic phonics, children are taught the whole word, and then analyse the separate parts (e.g. c-at). In synthetic phonics, they blend sounds together to produce (or "synthesise") the word. In other words, they learn the sounds first before putting these together to make words (c-a-t equals cat). I hope you're still with me!

I'm pretty certain that your child will be learning to read using synthetic phonics, so, if you want to help them, it's best if you use this method too. They will probably start using something very simple called "sound talk" where they listen to the sounds in a "CVC" word (sounds scary, but actually means consonant, vowel, consonant, like d-o-g) and then clap them out.

There are various different phonics programmes, including the Government's own one (which schools are encouraged to use, but don't have to). It has been very much influenced by others such as Jolly Phonics with its accompanying CD and songs, and Read Write Inc by Ruth Miskin (a former headteacher). Your child's school may use a mixture of different phonics programmes.

> "What I want the child to understand is that a letter is a speech sound written down. My big thing is that every child should learn to read, but you've got to have the sound knowledge before you can ask a child to read you a word."
>
> Ruth Miskin, creator of her own phonics scheme

Some children have a natural reading ability and seem to pick up reading almost by osmosis. You will know if you have one of these. For many others, synthetic phonics is now seen as the key to help them into the reading world.

> "My 5-year-old is now learning the sounds and is already starting to read and write, by sounding out the words as she goes. Once they get to blended sounds it all seems to click into place and off they go. Personally I think it is an excellent system."
>
> Natalie, mother of two daughters, aged 7 and 5

Because English is not the easiest language to learn (those 44 sounds from only 26), it takes time for your children to be taught to read. How they learn may also seem a bit random (although, clearly it's not!).

At first, your child will probably be taught a few letter sounds and these may not be the most obvious ones to you (children often learn s-a-t-p-i-n at the beginning). Some sounds (for example, ee, oa, ou, ng) are represented by two letters or even three. These are known as digraphs or trigraphs (some schools are official enough to use these intimidating sounding names, and you may also hear them mention the word grapheme, which just means the shape of the letter). You will (hopefully) find out what your child is up to by reading the school newsletter or asking the teacher. Then you can help. For example, if your child is learning "ee" as in sleep, you can build on this, by suggesting other words which contain that sound (need, feet, seed etc).

Phonics can be confusing for children, because some of the same sounds are represented by different groups of letters (ay and ai, for example). They will learn one of these at a time, so as not to complicate matters too much. I remember my son writing down "mum I love yoo" on a piece of paper which his teacher proudly showed me. She was delighted that he remembered the "oo" sound (even though the spelling of the word was wrong!).

I recently came across some fantastic online videos from primary-school teacher Christopher Thorne. They are a wonderful introduction to phonics, for children and parents, and I definitely recommend a look. Mr Thorne also shows you how to pronounce each of the letter sounds. See http://mrthornedoesphonics.com.

Learning through play

The learning through play ethos continues with phonics as there are often rhymes or songs to help with learning letters. Your child may also write in the air with "magic pens", or make "silly soup" choosing objects that begin with the same sound and putting them in a bowl. As they progress, they may play "word bingo". You could try these at home too.

What are the tricky words my child tells me about?

Your child may appear with a list of apparently harmless words on it. Don't be fooled, these are the "tricky" words (sometimes known as "sight words") which he will just have to learn (that is memorise). This is because they are very common, but difficult to sound out. More words will be added each term.

Tricky words include: the, he, she, was, to, you, said, my, no, all, going, away, come.

Warning: if your child is put on the Oxford Reading Tree scheme (the ones with Biff and Kipper), you will find that not all the words are phonetic. It's more of a sight-based scheme. Yes, this is rather odd (I often wonder if children are given these books just because the school already has them and doesn't want to buy new ones). This basically means you may have to help your child with some of the words as they are impossible to decode.

Some schools now follow the Rigby Star scheme. I've heard that these books are far more interesting.

Writing

This is another issue which can get parents - and children - worked up. Of course, writing is hugely important - in the long run, but it's not really that important when your child is aged 4. It comes with time and also requires more than brain power.

To be able to write properly, your child needs good fine motor skills. These really differ from child to child, although it's more common that boys find writing hard. As one Reception class teacher told me, "The girls sit and colour in, but the boys zoom around playing games and tend to do better with their numeracy."

"We encourage children to write and it's good to get them to do any kind of writing - it doesn't matter what – any kind of mark is good. We want them to become comfortable with this before we worry too much about holding the pencil correctly and forming the letters correctly.

Ruth Vered, Reception class teacher ”

Some teachers worry a lot about what they call the “correct pencil grip”. However, some children simply aren’t ready for this in Reception – they don’t have the motor skills yet. You should ask your teacher for her opinion on this. My son’s teacher was laid back about it, and right to be. He’s now in Year 1 and holds the pencil beautifully.

When your child starts school, he is unlikely to be doing much writing. Instead he may “draw” in the sand, with chalk or with glitter, or make shapes in the air with his finger. You can definitely help at home with similar activities. Finger painting is also good (albeit messy).

If your child is having real problems, you could ask the school to provide some good pencil grips for your child (they may do this already). You can also buy these online. Stabilo have some very good pencils for helping children to grip correctly and make it easier for them to write with (see www.stabilo.com). You could also try a triangular pencil.

Your child may find it physically hard to hold a pencil because his muscles are not yet developed enough. You can work on this with things like playdough, plasticine or threading (see p. 43), or even by buying a small ball which he can squish. Colouring books are also good.

To help your child practise writing, there are loads of books you can buy and many contain traceable letters. If you want to just write out letters yourself, do make sure that you do this the way the school wants you to – and always start with your pencil at the top to form letters. If you are looking for useful books, I would particularly recommend *abc doodles* by Nancy Meyers (Buster Books, 2010). It’s good fun as well as educational.

One of the most wonderful things about your child learning to write is the writing adventures they take. You may find that they present you with a "story" which is almost impossible to decipher. Soon, you will be able to work out some of the words (they will be written phonetically, which doesn't necessarily mean correctly). Interpreting their words reminded me of when my children started to talk, and only I understood them.

And if my child wants to write more?

It may be that your child finds writing easy and is desperate to write more. This can actually cause problems in Reception, as the Early Years curriculum is not designed for children to sit down at tables and do this. In fact, as one teacher said to me, "We would get into trouble if we had our 5-year-olds sitting down with pens and paper."

Instead of doing it formally, children are given "opportunities" for writing in different areas of the curriculum. For example, if they are role-playing that they work in a restaurant, they can take down orders.

It's possible that your child might become frustrated by this. If so, you should, as usual speak to the teacher, particularly as there may be more ways to introduce these "writing opportunities" into the curriculum. If this is not the case, then you could take your request to the headteacher. If that fails, you may simply have to look at Reception as a time for developing your child's social skills and learning in other areas, and work on his writing in your own time.

However, be aware that the ability to write under your supervision is not exactly what schools are aiming for.

" I sometimes have parents who tell me that their children can write. But can they really, independently? This curriculum is about children being able to do things by themselves, so they become independent learners. Can your child really write without someone standing over him? Does he understand the purpose of writing?

Tanja Perez-Williams, Reception class teacher ”

PROBLEM SOLVING, REASONING AND NUMERACY

Maths is also not what it used to be. For one thing, its name has changed: your child no longer learns "maths" but, at least in the Early Years, "numeracy". For another, the way maths is taught is completely different. And that can be confusing for parents.

It's not just about sums. These days children do a lot of practical activities to help them to sort, match, count and compare. They look at three-dimensional shapes, length, mass and capacity. They learn about time (including yesterday and tomorrow), money and working out one more or one less, or the concept of doubling. They also play games (jumping on tiles with numbers on, for example, or singing number rhymes) and solve problems (how many toys you could buy with a certain amount of money, for example).

Okay, but what about numbersquares, numberlines or numberbonds?

Twenty-first century children use different ways of learning maths at school and these have their own "mathematical" vocabulary.

A *numberline* is exactly what it says it is – various numbers all laid out on a line. At the beginning, children use this to help learn addition and subtraction. They will soon learn that if they start at any number, then add or take away another, it leads to a different number. Yes, they could work this out in their heads (or on their fingers!), but the numberline makes it all visual – and is also useful later on when they learn more complicated sums.

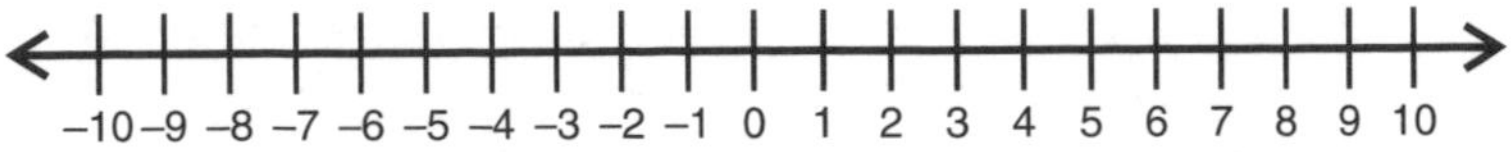

> "The beauty of using the number line is that children have a mental image of moving along it, and this can help those who struggle with abstract ideas. Many children soon grasp what is happening and no longer need the graphical image to support their thinking.
> Judy Sayers, senior lecturer in Mathematics Education at the University of Northampton"

They may also use a *numbersquare* to find the differences between bigger numbers. This is simply a square with numbers in rows going up from 1 to 100.

Your child may mention learning his *numberbonds* up to 10. This simply means the pairs of numbers which add up to 10: in other words, 9+1, 8+2, 7+3, 6+4, 5+5. You can make up numberbonds for any number, but in Reception, it's usually just up to 10.

Bear in mind that while you may find your child's maths confusing, they may feel the same about yours! If you ask them to "take away" or "subtract" a number, they may not understand you. That's because they're learning to "count back" instead. Similarly they will call addition "counting on".

The idea behind these new methods is to help develop mathematical thinking and "support" children's understanding of the number system (rather than just get them to answer questions). However, you may find that, if you have a child who is very good at numbers (and does them in his head), he may slow down when told to use a numberline.

The "learning goals" for early school maths range from sorting objects and recognising patterns, to recognising numbers up to 10 (or at the highest level, up to 20). You may scoff at these targets, and certainly many children go beyond these by the time they finish Reception. But schools do realise this - they will often separate children into groups, so some do more challenging work (counting in 2s or 10s, for example).

PERSONAL, SOCIAL AND EMOTIONAL DEVELOPMENT

This is all about how your child can work, play and co-operate with others. The idea is to help him become more self-confident and develop his social skills.

At the beginning of the school year, the main focus in this area will probably be about starting school, making friends and developing independence in the classroom. But it's also about sharing, taking turns, being sensitive to others and working as part of a group.

KNOWLEDGE AND UNDERSTANDING OF THE WORLD

The concept behind this is to help children make sense of the world they live in. It involves a mixture of history, geography, science and technology, as well as some religious education.

Reception class children might use magnifying glasses or binoculars, grow seeds, talk about the weather and seasons or visit the zoo. They could design a robot or a computer, talk about their own families or discuss different religious festivals.

One of the most popular (and common) topics under this heading is mini-beasts, which is basically learning about bugs such as ladybirds, worms or caterpillars. Young children seem to love exploring for these little creatures (some schools have their own mini-beast gardens!) and the topic can take in all sorts of areas of the curriculum including numeracy (counting insect legs/spots on ladybirds), literacy (stories about bugs) and creative development (making your own pictures/collages). It often involves planting too.

CREATIVE DEVELOPMENT

The intention behind this is to develop imagination, but also to work on the ability to communicate and express feelings and ideas creatively.

This area can be hugely enjoyable for children as it has so much scope to it. Children may do anything from making a musical instrument to designing a flag. They will also use role-play, listen and tell stories, sing, dance and do art (many find it difficult when they move into Year 1, where there is far less of this).

PHYSICAL DEVELOPMENT

This is better known by most of us as PE. And there is less of it than when many of us were at school – usually only two hours a week. This can be frustrating for many sporty children, but doesn't usually become a problem in Reception, partly because there is quite an emphasis on outside activities as well as inside.

Your child will probably use various pieces of equipment, throw, catch and do some team games. The learning goals also put a great emphasis on "movement", and in particular "moving with confidence, imagination and in safety". I'm assured that teachers make it more interesting than it sounds!

WHAT ELSE DO YOU NEED TO KNOW?

It's worth finding out about your school's reward programme, if only to be able to produce the right responses when your child talks about them ("You got the golden sash this week? Darling, that's fantastic!").

These really differ from school to school. They may be something obvious (a sticker for the "star of the week") or they may be a bit more complicated than that (one common theme is to have a sun and grey cloud scenario. Children are put on the grey cloud if they misbehave and on the sun if they are good). Schools can be really bad at explaining these set-ups, so ask at parents' evening if you want to know more.

If it's nearing the end of the year and your child seems to have been missed out when it comes to weekly recognition, it may be worth a quiet word with the teacher.

> "Everyone will do something amazing at some point and you need to give everyone a go. I do try to make sure everybody gets a reward."
> Debra Vaughan, Reception class teacher

How can you help?

Teachers may not love pushy parents, but they do love parents who reinforce learning at home (yes, it's a thin line, and I'm not quite sure where it's drawn).

My top tip here would be to read with your child regularly as it makes such a difference.

But there are so many other things you can also do – being creative (using pencils, crayons, beads and scissors); counting things at home, pointing out odd and even numbers (for example, on different sides of a street); singing number rhymes or playing games with dice. You could also talk about different festivals or countries. Most of this is pretty obvious!

SHOW AND TELL

At some point, your child may mention "show and tell". Inherited from the USA, this involves a small group of children (a different set each week) bringing in something from home which they would like to talk about. Some schools have strict rules on what a child can bring in (nothing edible, no toys) while others are open to almost anything (I think our only no-go was bringing in anything alive!).

It's a nice idea for the children, as it helps with their speaking and listening skills and confidence. However, you will feel absolutely awful if you forget to send something along, so write down when your child's group is having their turn and try very hard to put something in the bookbag the day before (otherwise you risk being a bad mum or dad).

CIRCLE TIME

This is another common school experience which probably wasn't around in your day (we weren't quite as into all this touchy-feely stuff then. . .).

As the name suggests, circle time occurs when all the children sit in a circle facing each other. This means it is always possible to maintain eye-contact.

Its aim is to teach children social skills and boost their confidence. It's also a great way to get them to speak and listen to each other, and also to sort out any problems. The children will be taught any circle time rules to follow - such as not to interrupt each other - and it gives them a proper turn to say what they want.

Circle time will continue as your child moves up the school. It can also be used in a variety of different ways - to have fun and discuss a particular issue, or to sort out a problem such as bullying.

PLAYTIME

Playtime can be a huge issue at school, despite its harmless-sounding name. This is a time when kids can be happy and play, but also when trouble can start, particularly because supervising vast numbers of children in a playground can be very tricky.

Your child will have at least two separate playtimes a day – sometimes three. The aim of playtime, of course, is for children to have a break from the structure of the school day (although the Early Years curriculum has far less structure), and also to play outside and make new friends. Some schools have playgrounds with brilliant equipment, and even invite special play leaders in to help with the younger children. At others, children are pretty much left to their own devices, and form into little groups. You may find that the boys go off and play football, for example – and if your son is not a "football boy" he may feel left out.

As mentioned earlier (in chapter 6), some schools have friendship benches and also older children (buddies) who can make sure your child is not left alone. Some also allow children to bring in skipping ropes (make sure you name these) or marbles to use at playtime, but others will only allow them to use school equipment. As there may not be enough of this to go round, children can soon get bored.

> "My daughter loved school right from the start, but she sometimes struggled with playtime. She would come home telling me stories of children telling others they couldn't play with them or of being pushed around by older children. I think it sounds like a free for all at playtime and only the strongest survive!
> Karen, mother of a daughter aged 8 and a son aged 7"

Many schools have separate playgrounds for the younger children (either just for Reception, or for the infant children) and take good care to settle the children during playtimes.

Schools often have "lunchtime supervisers" on duty during playtime, but many also have teachers – who know the children better, and are therefore more effective at crowd control. Some children may argue over simple things like what games to play, while others can be really unpleasant to each other. Although we might not like to admit it (and definitely not of our own child) small children can be manipulative and obnoxious. The more intelligent ones display this behaviour in the playground rather than in the classroom, where it could easily be stamped on.

> " The majority of friendship issues happen in the playground, because it's really difficult to monitor. When you're on duty, you can't see everything that happens, but if you think there is a problem with your child, you should definitely speak to the class teacher about it. She can ask the person on duty to keep an eye on the situation.
>
> Debra Vaughan, Reception class teacher

The playground is also a place where school crazes (Silly Bandz, Match Attax cards, etc.) can start. In a way this is just because it gives the children something to do. Some parents (and I tend to agree) really think there is a need for children to be taught playground games (the kind we used to play at school, for example Stuck in the Mud). Many have no idea what to do when given a long block of time outside, with no organisation.

> " We had some playground trouble and my son definitely found it difficult to make playground friends. One thing that helped was to send in a little toy

with him each day. That seemed to attract other children. And, although he's not the life and soul of the party, after a while, some kids just came over to play with him anyway. ”
Emma, mum of three, aged 6, 4 and 2

By the end of the school year, I think you'll be amazed by how much your child has learned, both socially and academically. They'll have had lots of fun, but somehow picked up a lot of information too. And then they'll no longer be the babies of the school. Instead they'll be getting ready for Year 1.

WALES, NORTHERN IRELAND AND SCOTLAND

The Early Years curriculum in Wales and Northern Ireland is very similar to that for England. One major difference (not relevant in Reception) in Wales is that the "learning through play" concept is now taken through to the age of 7.

The Scottish curriculum

Scotland has recently implemented a new curriculum called the Curriculum for Excellence. The idea is to ensure that "every child should experience a broad education", and there is a big focus on literacy and numeracy as well as the promotion of an active and healthy lifestyle (including so-called "risky play" like climbing trees!).

The new curriculum runs from age 3 to 18 (from nursery, all the way through the school years), and like the ones in England, Wales and Northern Ireland, it's play-based. When your child starts school, as in England, he will be following a curriculum (Early Level) which is for nursery and Primary 1.

The Scottish Government says that it has four aims or "capacities" for the curriculum: to help every child become "a successful learner, confident individual, responsible citizen and an effective contributor."

The new curriculum is divided into eight subject areas - expressive arts, health and well-being, languages, mathematics, religious and moral education, sciences, social studies and technologies.

Unlike the English curriculum, there is no set policy guidance on the use of phonics (even though it is frequently used).

For more on the Scottish education system and its new curriculum, visit www.ltscotland.org.uk.

9

Food at school

Once you're a parent, food takes on an entirely new significance. Many parents – myself included – have agonised over feeding their children. It's such a responsibility, not to mention hard work, but can meet with the most upsetting of responses ("yuck!" being far too common in many toddler lexicons). So, food at school is a huge issue. It's also a continuation of the tussle between giving your child more independence, whatever the consequences ("I had chips and apple crumble today") or retaining some control ("Did you enjoy the delicious packed lunch I made you?").

Most schools offer the choice of a hot dinner (sometimes, but not always cooked on the premises) or let children bring in a packed lunch from home. Very often all the infants eat together in the school hall or canteen, but Reception children usually come in first, so they won't have to queue up for too long.

SCHOOL DINNERS VERSUS PACKED LUNCHES

When weighing up your options, do take into account that schools may try to persuade you that it's in your child's best interest to take school dinners. This is sometimes as much to do with keeping the prices down (schools often want as many children as possible to eat school dinners) as what's best for your little one. The quality of school dinners can vary dramatically between schools. You need to think this one through carefully.

You also need to consider what kind of child you have when it comes to eating. Have you got a real fusspot or one who's open to all kinds of foods? Will your child actually eat what's on offer if you opt for school dinners?

> "I'd always go for school dinners over packed lunches, partly because it's so much less work for me! But I also think that school dinners offer greater variety and a more 'rounded' meal. They seem to encourage children to try new things. My daughter is open to all manner of dishes at school. She's even got a taste for curry – I could never have persuaded her to even try it!
>
> Debbie, mother of three children, aged 7, 5 and 2"

> "I try not to allow the children to have school dinners. It's usually junk and horrid. There was a huge campaign about healthy eating, which was great, but now things like hamburgers, doughnuts and iced cakes are on the menu again. You have so much more control over what they eat if they have packed lunches.
>
> Jayne Howarth, mother of a daughter, 11, and a son, aged 9"

There are, of course, advantages and disadvantages to both. Let's look at them in turn.

Five advantages of school dinners

1) There will be lots of choice

Packed lunches can soon become boringly repetitive.

2) Choosing his own meal helps make your child independent

There is something particularly grown-up about the thought of your small child choosing what he wants to eat and negotiating his way around a canteen with a tray in his hands.

3) The social aspect

Experts suggest that eating school dinners together is a good social experience for a child, and that it helps develop his table manners. (However, those with lunchboxes eat together too!)

4) Fussy eaters may be persuaded to try new foods. . .

and then carry this bravery into the food they eat at home. Peer pressure can work wonders. If a child sees a friend trying something, he may try it as well.

5) Helps concentration

Research by the School Food Trust suggests that children who eat a healthy cooked meal are more likely to concentrate in the afternoon.

You might want to wait and see what the canteen food is like before you sign your child up for school dinners (some forward-thinking schools arrange taster sessions). Or you could ask other parents (and their children) what they think of the food.

Ask if the teachers eat the school dinners – if they do, it tells you that the food is edible, at the very least.

Five disadvantages of school dinners

1) You can't control what your child is eating

Even if the school provides menus, this doesn't mean your child will choose what you would like him to.

2) Your child might eat the same thing every day!

True, they are not supposed to do this, as menus change and the options might sound terrific. However, your 4-year-old may not be able to read the menu, will soon forget what you told him to eat that morning, and then find it difficult to make a decision quickly when asked. Instead he may choose pasta or baked beans each lunchtime.

3) Not enough fruit and veg

Although schools are supposed to offer nutritionally balanced meals, your child may not choose the right options. No one will force him to eat his vegetables!

4) Waste of money?

If your child doesn't eat what's on offer (or just has a slice of bread and a boiled egg each day) it is a waste of money.

5) Yucky food

If the food is (in the words of one 4-year-old) "horrid", your child won't eat it. So packed lunches are the only alternative.

The quality of school lunches can really vary, not just across the country, but from school to school. Some will be really enthusiastic about quality food, perhaps even growing their own vegetables in the school garden. Others offer low quality stodge.

“I'd recommend that parents should find out if their school has its own kitchen. We don't have the

capacity to cook at our school, and although it's a balanced menu, the meals are not the best. In fact, because we don't have the money to invest in our kitchen facilities, our school lunches are still not good enough and on occasions embarrassing!
Hugh Greenwood, Headteacher of Boughton-under-Blean and Dunkirk Primary School"

HEALTHY EATING

Modern schools often talk about "encouraging" healthy eating. Sometimes, in a canteen which offers smiley faces and potato waffles as "vegetables", this can seem like lip service.

However, there are now national nutritional standards for school lunches. Food has to be healthier (lower in fat, salt and sugar; more grilling and less frying) than it was previously, and schools must provide at least one portion of fruit and vegetables per pupil each day. In addition, chocolate, sweets, salty snacks and sugary drinks are not allowed.

Many parents feel that school lunches have definitely got better since chef Jamie Oliver began his campaign to improve them. The School Food Trust was set up in 2005 with a remit to "transform school food" and sets a number of standards which you can see on its website, www.schoolfoodtrust.org.uk.

"A few years ago, we were allowed to see the ingredients list for the food which the children were being given. It was absolutely shocking, particularly the oddments of meat that were being used! Things have massively improved since then, but I'm still careful. I allow the children to have school dinners twice a week as a treat. ”

David, father of two

One problem with the new dinners is that some children won't eat the food! Teachers or lunchtime supervisors may try to be encouraging, but they can't do much more than that.

“ You can put a sprout on a plate, but a child will refuse to eat it! There is also a real divide between those children who will have a proper meal later and those who won't. These children need to eat a good meal at lunchtime, so it matters what you put in front of them. ”

Julia Skinner, ex-primary school headteacher

PACKED LUNCHES

If you opt for packed lunches, you may find that inspiration soon deserts you. And if you have a fussy eater, you may end up making the same thing (cheese sandwiches, anyone?) every day.

In my experience, children don't like to stand out - or at least not very much. They might accept some vegetables with their lunch (my daughter used to happily munch her way through a little pot filled with carrot, cucumber and pepper) but could find it embarrassing if you pop in a bento box filled with tuna rice salad and fresh tomato and chilli salsa (it has happened, apparently). It's easy to find suggestions for great, healthy, packed lunches, but you might also find that your child won't actually eat them - hardly the point if you have chosen this option to ensure they will gobble up what they're given.

> "Why the obsession with chicken or tuna? What is wrong with salmon, eggs, tahini, hummus and rocket, avocado and prawns, roasted vegetables, mozzarella and tomato? You can make lunches as exciting as your imagination. Just giving a child cheese or tuna mayo sandwiches each day; no wonder they don't like to eat them!"
>
> Olivia, mother of two girls, aged 10 and 5

Tips for livening up lunchboxes

- Simple changes – make sandwiches with different types of bread like pitta.
- Try out different fillings (but don't be surprised if your child then asks for tuna or cheese, again). How about some dips (hummus or tsatziki) with raw carrot sticks?
- Oatcakes, rice cakes and dried fruit are good alternatives to processed, high-fat, sugary snacks.
- Put in some fruit and don't always make it an apple! Why not give your child a fruit pot of melon or grapes?

Most schools do not refrigerate packed lunches, so invest in a cool pack, especially if you are sending in meat or fish sandwiches.

If you decide to be a bit more adventurous, go slowly. Don't try something too different from the usual, and choose something which won't actually scare off your child – a pot of pasta or rice, or pitta pockets, for example. Try to include a combination of different kinds of food – carbohydrates (bread, rice), protein (chicken, salmon) and fruit or vegetables.

> "All I can say from experience is that if you try to give your child something you know they are not going to eat, it's going to end up in the bin at school. Then your child will be left in the sorry situation of having to ask schoolmates for some of their food (and some schools don't even allow sharing!). It's not worth it."
>
> Becky

Some parents say they choose to give their Reception-aged child a packed lunch to make life easier for him. The child will then have something familiar to turn to at lunchtime, and won't have to choose a main meal or carry around a tray. However, I would suggest asking your child what they actually want to do – they may want the chance to choose their food and be like everyone else (or they find this a terrible idea and want to stick with mummy or daddy's sandwiches).

Just because you have chosen to give your child packed lunches in Reception doesn't mean you have to do this for ever. You can change your mind, although you may have to give notice of any move. Make a decision based on what you *and* your child want. If it's going to drive you insane to make a packed lunch each day, don't do it! Perhaps you could compromise on one or two days a week.

Remember to label your child's lunchbox and any items which aren't disposable such as their drinking bottle or cutlery. Buy a non-spill bottle and easy to open lunchbox (you don't want your child not to be able to get to their food!)

The "lunchbox police"

Don't think, just because you've chosen to give your child a packed lunch, that this means you alone choose what to put into it. Schools love to stick their noses in here too.

There are often rules about what your child can, and can't, take in his school lunchbox. These are generally quite straightforward, connected to a healthy-eating policy and allergy awareness (no chocolate, no nuts).

But some schools are very specific with lists of "banned" foods. I heard of one which allowed plain or fruit cake but not chocolate cake. Another wrote to parents saying that they "expected" the children's packed lunch to include "a drink, sandwiches, fruit and/or a yoghurt" - not much room for creativity there. It also asked them to "please remember our healthy Packed Lunch Policy" - crisps, chocolate or sweets, fizzy drinks, nuts, and jam or chocolate spread in sandwiches were not allowed. "If these items are found in your child's lunchbox, they will be returned to you at the end of the school day," wrote the school's headteacher. Doesn't he sound like a friendly chap?

It's the school's duty to tell you about any rules or regulations they have, but it's your duty to stick to them.

Some parents hate the idea of the school telling them what they should feed their children. Others find it galling that the school won't allow them to send in a biscuit with their child's lunch, but will serve ice-cream and potato waffles to children having school dinners.

> "When the school told me not to send in a treat (a small slice of healthy homemade cake) with my son's lunch, I was irritated. I told them that when they stopped serving doughnuts for school dinners, I'd stop sending in cake!"
>
> "No idea"

Despite all the talk of healthy lunchboxes, some schools can be lax when it comes to enforcement. This can create its own problems. . .

> "My son occasionally takes a packed lunch to school and is more than happy with healthy sandwiches

and fruit and water. But the minute more than a couple of children have chocolate or crisps in their lunchboxes I get nagged that it's not fair and he's missing out. I find this a real pain. ”
Nicola, mother of one son, aged 6

“ I do lunch duty every day at the primary school where I work, so I get to see what children bring in their lunchboxes – some are just awful. How can you expect a child to concentrate if you load them full of additives/preservatives/colouring and sugar?! Yesterday a 7-year-old in my class had a bag of crisps, two lollies, a large gingerbread man, a ketchup sandwich and a cheap fruit drink. He has this almost every day and his parents wonder why he gets in trouble for messing around in class or being so tired in the afternoon that he can't focus on anything. ”
Michelle

An empty lunchbox doesn't mean your child has eaten everything in it. He may have thrown away the bits he didn't fancy, or swapped them with friends. And, of course, he may choose not to share this information with you.

LUNCHTIME PROBLEMS

Young children can find eating at school a little intimidating and noisy. They might also find it genuinely difficult to carry a tray and

choose what to eat. This means that, although you have signed them up for school lunches, they may not actually eat them.

You can help by ensuring your child gets used to eating with others before he starts school. When it comes to Reception-aged children, the staff often help out, encouraging them to eat or helping to cut up their food. But if you are concerned, you should mention this to your teacher, so that she can then keep a closer eye on what's going on.

> "It's worth bearing in mind that children tend to eat painfully slowly at school as there are so many people to chat to. Having friends around slows them down even more. And of course time is limited. This is definitely something worth tackling at home via games, bribes or threats!"
>
> Cathy Beck, primary school teacher

One little boy I know hated lunchtimes because his friends finished their food quickly and then left to play outside without him. Do ask your child if there are any problems and think about how you (and the school) could improve matters.

What if you want to change the food on offer?

What our children eat really matters. If you aren't happy with the food your child is being served, don't just give up. You - and other parents - have the power to change things, if you put your minds to it. However, you must go about this constructively. Headteachers don't mind parents who are positive and have plans for change rather than just complaints.

Jackie Schneider was one of a group of parents who was instrumental in changing the food which was offered to children in the London borough of Merton. They were determined to persuade the local authority that the current provision was substandard.

> “At my children's primary school the food was very poor quality and differed enormously from the menus parents were shown. In addition the food often ran out, with children being given half sized portions to make it go further. On occasion the food was burnt and apples were served up brown having been sliced earlier in the day.
> Jackie Schneider, mother of three and school food campaigner”

Jackie and other parents persuaded the caterers to change the way they prepared food, and also to follow stricter nutritional standards. They kept a detailed food diary, wrote to teachers and governors, contacted the local authority and showed them pictures of what the children were being served. They also got in touch with the local paper. Jamie Oliver's school meals campaign also helped as, in Jackie's words it "shone a spotlight on the issue". The result was new caterers and far better school meals.

If you are a parent who wants to make a change, you could follow Jackie's lead. If you don't actually want to run an action group, you could simply speak to your teacher or headteacher, as well as the governors (ask if they have eaten the school lunches and what they thought). Each state school should have a teacher and governor who have healthy eating as part of their remit. You could also write to the catering company, local councillors or the local authority.

How can you help choose what they eat at school?

Most schools now provide advance details of what's going to be on offer. They might send these via email or put them onto their website. For a number of schools, this information is provided in order for you to show the menus to your children and discuss what they might eat at school. However, some schools ask you to pick what your child is going to eat in advance. He will then be provided with a sticker or wristband so that the lunchtime staff know what to give him.

I found that, when my son just appeared to be eating boiled eggs every day, what helped was sitting down and looking at the menu with him. We then chose his menu for the whole week and gave it to the teacher. She reminded him of these choices each day.

PAYING FOR THE FOOD

Some schools ask you to pay for school lunches in advance (weekly, monthly or termly), usually by cheque. Others still ask children to bring in money every day. This can be a real pain, as it's problematic to remember and also means relying on a young child not to lose the coins you've given him.

> “When my oldest son started school, he had to get used to taking £1.85 to school each day. It is always such a hassle to find the change, and if you just give it to them to put in their pocket, I find that it evaporates! I'd definitely recommend giving your child a wallet or purse to put the money in. And make sure you label it clearly with their name.
>
> Ellen Arnison, mother of three boys, aged 10, 8 and 14 months”

Some schools collect the named purses or wallets each morning and keep them in the classroom until lunchtime. This means there's far less opportunity for these to get lost.

Other schools have introduced different ways of solving this problem. One solution is a cashless system, whereby parents and/or children can put credit onto an account and swipe a card in the canteen. This can also be used to give a report on a child's purchase, which can then be passed back to his parents.

Of course, the upside of paying for food on the day means that you have the flexibility to choose between school meals and packed lunches. Find out what system your school runs.

GOING HOME FOR LUNCH

In the old days, when I was young, many children went home at lunchtimes. In fact, I remember wandering around the playground sadly (feel free to shed a tear) because my best friend, Alison, wasn't around to play with. Instead I had school dinners – and Alison used to smuggle me chips when she came back to school in the afternoon.

These days, going home at lunchtime is far more unusual (except of course, in the early days, when your child may not be staying for afternoon classes yet). But there's often no reason why, in principle, a child should not go home. If this appeals to you, then you should ask the teacher or headteacher. However, think carefully about this.

Ultimately, whether you want your child to be in or out of school at lunchtime has to be your decision. It's certainly true that some teachers – and parents – feel that children need to be in school at this time, to make friends and develop their social skills. But some parents love that extra contact in the day, and feel that it's truly needed. Others use it for specific reasons (one little boy I heard about used to leave school for lunch one day every week to eat with his grandma!).

> "I used to bring my daughter home for lunch when she first started school because she hadn't settled particularly quickly and it broke the day up for her. I'm sure it meant that she was happier to leave me in the morning because she knew she would be seeing me later on.
> Sally, mother of two daughters, aged 6 and 3"

Allergies

Many schools now have strict policies on allergies, especially when it comes to nuts (and sometimes sesame). This may mean that your child is not allowed to bring in anything at all – from peanut butter sandwiches to hummus – containing these banned foods. The school should let you know about this, but if you are unsure, you should check. Otherwise they may confiscate banned items from your child's lunchbox – leaving him hungry and irritated.

“I have two sons with nut allergies. If they eat nuts it means an adrenalin shot and a trip to hospital, at the least. They know that they can't eat nuts, but it's very hard as you can't monitor other children all the time. Because of this, I completely support the school when they make decisions like banning nuts. It's my children's lives at stake and I'm sorry if that means your child can't have peanut butter sandwiches.”

Kat, mother of three

OTHER FOOD AT SCHOOL

Food at school isn't only about lunches. Your child will have a daily snack and there will also be special food on birthdays as well as demands for something to eat at pick-up.

The daily snack

Children in the Infants (Reception, Year 1 and 2) at state schools are given a mid-morning snack (usually a piece of fruit) for free.

However, some children (the fussy ones) refuse to eat what's on offer, which means that you will be asked to bring something in.

You may, once again, find that there are rules about what is allowed – usually fruit or a fruit bar, perhaps a yoghurt or piece of cheese. Some schools do accept home-made biscuits and cakes, but try to stick to the school's healthy-eating policy as it makes things so much easier for the teachers, and is better for your children too.

When it comes to private schools, it varies as to whether snacks are provided or if parents are asked to bring them in. Children are usually asked to bring in a water bottle, named, of course.

After-school snacks

You'll probably find that your child will be "starving" after school. It's wise to bring in something with you for pick-up (it will also stop demands to purchase something at the local shop or ice cream van on the way home).

I honestly feel that parents should be able to choose their child's after-school snacks, but wouldn't recommend that you go for something particularly unhealthy every day. Try cheese, fruit (or dried fruit or fruit bars), or something like a rice cake, bread sticks or oat biscuit. Flapjacks are another filling alternative.

Birthday treats

Many schools allow children to bring in cakes or treats (do check) to mark a birthday. If this is the case at yours, it's something you should plan for, as children tend to love being the bearer of "special food".

These treats can be in cake or biscuit form. However, be aware that it's much, much simpler for the teachers if they are easy to hand out. This means that you will be in the staff's good books if you provide a cake which is already cut into slices, or individual fairy cakes or cookies. Remember to count the teacher and teaching assistant when you're figuring out quantities!

10

Time off school: illnesses and holidays

WHEN YOUR CHILD IS ILL. . .

Being around other children is excellent for developing social skills in your offspring. Unfortunately, it's also excellent for developing illnesses – as you may soon (sadly) find out.

> “I am sick of children in school passing on their bugs to my daughter, and eventually me. It's one thing that she has to be off sick because of someone else's slack parenting – it's quite another when I inevitably catch it too and have to spend even more time off work. Parents need to take responsibility for their kids and not use school as a daytime

dumping ground, especially when the children are covered in snot or spots!
Suzie, mother of one daughter ”

So, when should you send your child to school and when should you keep him at home? It may sound like an easy question, but there are three factors you will need to take into consideration.

- How ill is your child?
- Is there anyone available to look after him if he stays at home?
- Is there a danger that he will make other children ill if he goes to school?

How ill is your child?

As his parent, you probably know your child best. Some children will say they feel ill (often something simple like having a tummy ache) when they are perfectly capable of managing a day at school. At other times, your little one may seem tired and have a cough or cold. You feel he could do with a day at home. What should you do?

The general advice on this is to send your child into school if he isn't contagious. Some people advise that you should consider whether you would take a day off work if you had the condition your child has. If so, then you should keep him at home. You will also have to make a judgement as a parent on this (if your 4-year-old seems very under the weather and you think he will benefit from being warm and doing nothing for a day, then keep him off).

If your child has a temperature, and in particular if he is infectious and/or has been sick or had diarrhoea, you should definitely keep him away from other children (and their teachers). In fact, most schools have policies which ask you to keep a child away from the school for 24 or 48 hours after he's been sick. You can find out more about these policies via the school website, office, prospectus, or the information pack you will have been given when your child started school. If your child has an infectious illness such as chickenpox, mumps or conjunctivitis, or an unexplained rash, you must keep him off.

> “A mother in my son's class sent her daughter into school the day after she was sick all night. Guess what? The whole class got ill. . .”
> Terry

If you do decide to keep your child at home, you should definitely call the school, preferably by registration time, to say what's wrong. Most schools also ask for you to either write a note covering the absence (you can send this when your child returns) or to drop the school an email. Schools need to record why pupils aren't there. If your child is off school for more than a day or two (how many days will depend on the school policy), you may be asked for proof of their illness, such as a doctor's note.

Real or pretend illness?

Sometimes children will say they feel ill in order to stay off school, even though they are fine. This may be because they fancy some time at home with you, because they are tired, or for a more serious reason (they don't like their teacher or are having friendship problems).

With a young child, you can usually tell whether an illness is real. In any case, fakery will become increasingly obvious if it happens on a regular basis. If your child doesn't seem at all unwell, but is clearly keen to be off school for some reason, you need to address this by talking to him about it, and also speaking to his teacher. If you simply think your child is being cheeky, then you could agree that he stays off school, but lay some ground rules (he has to lie quietly in bed, and not watch TV/go on the computer or Nintendo DS). This should make it less likely that he wants to be at home in the future, unless he is genuinely unwell!

Is there anyone at home to look after your child?

A major reason why parents send unwell children to school is because they want to avoid taking time off work to care for them.

This is especially true if they don't have the option of working from home.

One recent study reported that half of the parents questioned sent their child to school when he was unwell (more worryingly, 20% admitted they sent them in when they knew they were contagious). The main reasons given were that the parents thought their child would "perk up" once at school, and also because work commitments and lack of childcare made it difficult to keep them off.

> "I have to hold my hands up and say that I have sent my children into school when I knew that they should be at home. I don't mean that they were vomiting, but they were hot and snotty and probably infected other children by being there. The problem is that I work part time and already feel that I'm seen as someone who's not fully committed to work. It's really hard for me to take extra days off because of my children."
>
> Joyce

If your child is ill, you need to think about his needs and *also* those of the other children in the class. If you have a partner, then perhaps you could ensure that he takes a day off to look after the child once in a while, or call in the grandparents (if they live nearby). Hopefully it won't be too common an occurrence.

Is there a danger that he will make other children ill if he goes to school?

This is another biggie, and regrettably, it's one which many parents ignore.

> "I can't believe how irresponsible parents are – and how unhygienic school ends up being. I'm sure that thousands of school days are lost each year because one parent decides to send their child into a classroom of otherwise healthy pupils. Don't parents know when it's time to keep a child home from school? Where is the awareness or any sign of thinking about others? It's good to teach children sharing, but most illnesses, like inappropriate toys, are better left at home. Please don't bring them to school.
>
> Grace, mother of a son aged 10 and daughter aged 7"

Other parents do not want their child to get ill because you sent yours to school when you shouldn't have. Teachers don't want to get ill either.

Trying to prevent infections

You can't wrap your child up in cotton wool, but you can do your best to help him keep healthy.

1) Tell him to wash his hands with soap.
2) Teach him how to blow his nose properly, to use a tissue (paper ones which can be binned are best) and to sneeze (and cough) into it.
3) Feed him healthy food – fruit and vegetables, and juice if he needs a Vitamin C boost.

Being sent home from school

School staff will ring a parent as soon as they recognise that a child needs to go home. In other words, it's probably pointless sending in your child if you know you are going to get that call. However, most schools won't ring you if it's near home-time.

It's the call which parents dread – the school office asking you to come and collect your child. And it's so much worse if you are at work and far away from the school (you risk being seen as an uncaring parent if you can't be there immediately), or if you're not convinced your child is ill at all.

Some schools allow you to speak to your child on the phone to find out what's wrong. This can be a blessing as it may be that the sore ear/wrist/leg is not really that bad and can wait until school pick-up time. But other schools are especially cautious and I've known a number of parents complain that they've had to pick up their child, and been surprised by how healthy he's appeared to be.

Note: Make sure your school has up-to-date contact details in case of emergency. And ensure that they have a few names of people who would be available to come to school quickly if needed (you and your partner, a local friend, grandparent or childcarer).

Attendance records

Schools are very keen to have high rates of attendance. They now have attendance targets which are regularly monitored and are also used as part of Ofsted inspections. This can mean they don't want children to take days off, even if they are unwell! I have heard of parents being rung by the school, asked where their child is, and if they can prove he is really ill.

“ At our school, when a child is now off school ill, the school asks for proof when they come back! This can be really tricky if you haven't taken them to the doctor. The school is absolutely neurotic about attendance, so if you don't have proof, your child is put down as having had an 'unauthorised' absence. Because of this I take my kids to school on every occasion unless they are really ill. I can't say that this is particularly good for them, but I don't like the idea that I'm being accused of doing something wrong or lying otherwise. ”

Deepa

Another problem is that children crave the stickers or even prizes which come with a full year's attendance. That means they want to go to school, even if they are unwell.

INSET days

Many parents have no idea what INSET days are for and just accept them as an extra day when the kids are around. However, these “In Service Training Days” aren't officially “holidays”. Instead, they consist of five extra days per year which are set aside for teachers to train. The idea is that they are an occasion for all staff to be brought together and keep skills and knowledge up to date.

It is a legal requirement for state schools to have INSET days, and some schools simply put them on the first or last day of a term or half-term (that way the staff have to come in, but the kids get an extra day off). Schools should give plenty of notice of dates, but some position them far more randomly, which can be a problem.

HOLIDAY TIME

School holidays are sent to try us. Yes, it's great to spend time with your children, but long holidays can stretch apparently endlessly into the future, and a few hours post-school childcare is pretty useless when the children are at home all day. Actual vacationing can also be extremely expensive. So, what can be done?

Naturally all schools have holidays, although some are longer than others (private schools, for example). This is because state schools are set a particular number of teaching days per academic year (190), and independent schools don't have to follow this. The local authority sets the term dates and holidays for community and voluntary controlled schools, while the governing body sets the dates for other state schools. Headteachers set the term and holiday dates for private schools.

The big issue: holidaying in term-time

Since I had children, it's become clear to me that my childless work colleagues and friends are more than happy that parents are limited to travelling in the school holidays. "Leave the beaches, cities and countryside of the world to the rest of us for a while," one friend told me. "I love the certainty that school holidays give me when it comes to planning my holidays."

And while holidays are transformed when you have kids (early mornings, self-catering, baby-sitters), the holidaying possibilities really change once those kids start school. Parents feel angry at being fleeced by travel companies (prices can go up by as much as 80% in school holidays), so more and more people are now taking holidays when their children should be at school, even though this is not supposed to happen.

Schools *hate* children being off school. As with illnesses, holidays affect attendance records and disrupt their learning (very possibly in that order!). The Education Act of 1996 states that parents have a "legal duty" to ensure their child attends school regularly, and schools generally only "authorise" term-time holidays if there are special reasons. Each request is looked at on its own merit and granting time off is entirely at the headteacher's discretion (usually after looking at a child's general attendance records).

> "At our daughters' primary school, they tell you that if you are gone for two weeks or more, they reserve the right to remove your child from the school register. You can go abroad if you like – you just might not have a school place when you get back."
>
> Rachael, mother of two

Different schools deal with term-time holidays in different ways, and some are more sympathetic than others. Your school may agree to a holiday request if your child's general attendance is high, above 95%. Alternatively, it may adopt a zero-tolerance line, whereby requests are rarely, if ever, granted. This doesn't mean that you can't go away – they can't physically hold onto your child while you try to remove him for your trip – but if you do, then this will count as an "unauthorised absence".

If you are thinking of taking your child out of school during term-time, ask the school as far in advance as possible. Schools are actually given discretion to grant up to 10 days' leave a school year if they believe it's justified (lower holiday costs don't count), and nothing will happen to you, or your child, if you take them out for the odd day (except that the school will be irritated).

You should note that state schools in England are also now allowed to fine families if the school feels they've had too many "unauthorised absences". The fixed penalty is £50 (which rises to £100 if it's not paid within 28 days). However, the fines often cost a lot less than the money saved by going on holiday in June, for example, rather than July. One headteacher told me that she had parents who give her the holiday request form, with a £50 cheque stapled on. This all creates tension between school staff and parents.

> "Regular attendance is really important. Apart from the 'formal' learning, there are heaps of experiences children miss if they're not there every

day such as forming friendships and getting to know the routines. A few weeks off may not seem too bad, but if they are the first few weeks of the year, your child will miss out on lots of important information. If they leave before the end of the year, they miss all the goodbyes which are important too. ”
Julia Skinner, ex-headteacher of a primary school

One major argument against taking children on holiday during term-time is, of course, that this disrupts their learning. But if a trip in term-time is the only chance that a child might have to go on holiday, is it worth it? Perhaps schools should use more discretion when it comes to the holidays suggested, weighing up a beach holiday against a more educational-sounding one to Rome or another city, for example.

Personally I don't think it matters very much if a young child misses a day or two of school. However, I wouldn't recommend it as I don't think it's a great lesson for a child – it seems to show that you don't value school and learning. I'm more opposed to parents taking children out of school when they're older. They could miss important work which they might find hard to catch up on.

Some people argue that term-times should vary across different local authorities, so that travel companies are bamboozled into a fairer pricing structure. But many parents argue against this, saying that, if they have children at different schools, this would be a nightmare. I'm not sure there is a solution.

“ I've taken my 5-year-old out of school twice now. At this stage in his schooling I cannot see that this will affect his education. In fact, I am concerned that if it is so detrimental to his education to miss five days of school then how much are we expecting kids to learn on a day by day basis? ”

Vicky

Is there ever a good time to go?

Some parents will always want to take holidays in term-time, whatever the consequences. If this is true of you, at least give the timing some thought, for example, by avoiding any special occasions (the school show) or exam periods. You could ask the headteacher whether she thinks there are any events simply not to be missed. The school will thank you for it (er, as well as being annoyed that you are going away in the first place!).

“ I can't condone parents taking children out of school, but I think there's room for both parents and headteachers to be realistic. I would recommend that parents should have a conversation with the headteacher and discuss if there are parts of the year when they should avoid going away. ”

Hugh Greenwood, Headteacher of Boughton-under-Blean and Dunkirk Primary School

“ Neither myself nor my husband could get time off over the summer holidays. Our only chance of going away or even spending any quality time together was to take my daughter out of school. Our request was denied, but we took her anyway! We will try not to do this again, but I have to say that we were told (in a nudge nudge, wink wink kind of way) that although it would count as unauthorised absence, this year's report had been 'done', and so the absence wouldn't be recorded. ”

Lily's mum

But they don't do anything in the last few weeks of term

When schools get angry about parents taking the odd day off for a holiday (missing the last day of term, for example), parents often retort that their kids don't do anything during this time anyway. And I'm afraid this is often true. You may be surprised by how much television gets watched in school during the last week of term.

“ Schools can be really unhelpful. We could have gone on holiday a week earlier, but the school decided to have its last school day on a Monday. It was pointed out that it would be a waste as so many families would take that week as holiday for the loss of one day, but the school went ahead anyway. On the day, the children just watched DVDs! From now on I'll do what's best for us – nothing really gets learnt at the end of a school year, partly as the children are so tired out anyway and need a break. ”

Carmella

Private schools

Independent schools have longer holidays than state schools (ironic, that parents are spending money and getting shorter terms!). They usually set these in line with local state schools and through liaising with other private schools in the area.

The longer holidays are partly because private schools have no statutory requirements to have a particular number of school days in a year, and partly for other reasons – some independent schools have longer days, some headteachers want longer holidays for themselves and their staff (though they won't tell you that!), and some parents know how to put on the pressure.

> “Our school changed their half term to a week earlier, so that we wouldn't get caught up in the hordes on the slopes! This was obviously due to parental pressure. The PTA at our school is very, very powerful and the headmaster is very accommodating.”
>
> "Yucky mum"

This can be both a boon and a problem. It's a boon because you can get away on holidays earlier and so miss the masses (and the rise in prices). However, because of the longer time period, it also means more childcare arrangements. Which leads me onto...

What can I do with the children during the holidays?

> “School holidays can be very hard, especially if you don't have any family nearby to help. My advice would

be to plan carefully, to do playdate swaps with friends and to ask your employer if you can adjust your hours slightly over the holidays if that will help. ”

Eleanor, mother of two sons, aged 7 and 4

It is lovely when your children are off school and you can spend time with them. But it's not so great if you need to work as well, nor for parents who don't work, when the holidays are so long. School holidays can be a real problem for parents who are busy on particular days. Suddenly you need full cover and it isn't always easy to find. That's why you need to plan ahead.

Find out if your local authority runs any play schemes (there may be information about these at your local library, the internet, or the Government's "Childcare Finder", http://childcarefinder.direct.gov.uk). Websites such as Netmums and Mumsnet (which have local sections) should also have information. There may even be a scheme at your child's school. These usually run during the equivalent of school hours or perhaps a little longer (9am until 4pm, for example) and offer a range of activities. They are also not too expensive. Some local councils offer free fun days too.

Other holiday play schemes can also be run by charities, private companies and religious organisations, and there are lots of them available. Your school may have details of some of these, but otherwise you should be able to find out from word of mouth and also internet searches. These days, holiday clubs span anything from cookery to karate but they can be expensive (upwards of £100 for a week). They usually run in school-type hours, but some offer extended care for working parents. Some camps offer a half-day option which can be good for younger children.

“ School holidays can be a source of aggravation, to be honest. It sounds like a terrible thing to say as it makes it appear that you don't want to be with your children. That isn't it: it's just that the school holidays are so long. Where I live there are plenty of schemes available – and some are very good value. Walsall Council had a sports scheme during the summer holidays. It cost just £8 per day – and the children enjoyed it.

Jayne Howarth, mother of a daughter, 11, and a son, aged 9 ”

You need to think about whether your child will enjoy a holiday scheme. Some children love organised activities, and others hate them. Some children also get very worried about going to a camp where they won't know anyone else, so it's wise to speak to other parents and see if you can arrange for your child to go with a friend.

Remember that your child may be really tired after a long term or year at school. He may need some time off before launching into a holiday camp (although obviously this depends on having someone to look after him).

Other holiday options include sorting out a childcare rota with friends or family, and making sure, if possible, that both parents spend some time with the kids. If you have younger children, you could see if any childcare they have can be extended to your older ones.

“ I work part time, and have one child at school, with another at a childminder. I had no idea what to do when my son had his first extended holiday from school, but my childminder was amazing. She basically took him as well as the younger one and it worked really well. Now it's a regular arrangement.

Pippa ”

Keep learning

When school's out, learning probably isn't at the top of your summer to-do list. Well, perhaps you should think again. Don't you know that the summer break can actually damage your child's brain. . .?

Apologies if I'm making you paranoid, but recent research from Johns Hopkins University (in the USA) suggested that "summer learning loss" can be a real problem if parents fail to keep their children "mentally active". Various organisations are now trying to persuade parents to sign up for summer programmes to make sure their children don't fall behind. I'm not too sure of this.

Of course the issue does make some sense. If we adults didn't work for six weeks, we would probably also lose our edge. But we are talking about children here, and many would argue that they simply need some time off. When children are very little, they need to recharge their batteries and not learn all the time.

> "There is no doubt that children learn stuff in school and forget it when they're not in school. There is a dip. But when it comes to seeing how serious that is and how quickly a child can make it up, then that's a very difficult question to answer.
>
> Dylan Wiliam, Emeritus Professor at the Institute of Education"

What's particularly interesting about the research in this area is that it's reading aptitude which seems to drop the most. This is, of course, something which parents could easily address themselves simply by encouraging their children to read over the summer. And that's something I would definitely recommend. Your child could also make a scrapbook of what he's been up to. However, don't forget that children need time to play and to entertain themselves. They also learn just by meeting other people, going to museums and foreign countries (hearing other languages, using a different currency). Try not to get too caught up in competitive educating during vacation time!

11

When your child may be the only one

Sometimes school can be very hard – and the cause is more complicated than your child not getting an invite to a birthday party or disliking school dinners. It can, unfortunately, be a real struggle. In this chapter, we'll look at situations when your child may feel left out. Differences can cover anything from shyness to special needs and, although I can't wave a magic wand, I hope the advice below helps.

IS YOUR CHILD VERY SHY?

As your child gets used to being at school, he will, hopefully, blossom, make friends and have fun. However, this could be harder if he is shy.

A shy child may hate asking questions or standing up in front of others, which will make lessons (and particularly show and tell) difficult. He may also feel very self-conscious and find it hard to make friends. How can you help? After all, you don't want him to go through life missing opportunities and not having fun.

Five don'ts when it comes to shyness

1) Don't judge your child

Accept that he may take his time in new situations and don't make an issue of it.

2) Don't label him

Don't describe your child as "very shy" either when you're talking to, or about, him. Labels can become self-fulfilling. Try not to let other people (teachers, parents of friends) label him either. If you need to come up with a description, suggest that he likes to "think things through".

3) Don't do everything for him

Your child needs to learn to do things (and speak up) for himself. Otherwise he can't develop his confidence.

4) Don't give up

If he says he doesn't want to go to a party or playdate, ask him why, and perhaps suggest he tries to go along to an event every so often.

5) Don't apologise for him

Shy and quiet children often make a few close friends, are great listeners and can be deep thinkers! If you apologise for your child you may make him overly concerned that shyness is something very negative.

> "You need to build up your child's self-confidence first, for example by suggesting that he tries a new activity and then praising his efforts. Shy children often worry a lot and are concerned that someone will laugh at them if they make mistakes. Tell him

that it's okay to get things wrong – that's how you learn. And let him know that you don't always find everything easy to start with too. ”

Sue Atkins, parenting expert

It's helpful if you can take note of *when* your child is shy. Is it all the time, or only in certain situations? Once you can be a bit more specific, it should be easier to help.

Children learn from watching other people, especially their parents. Even if you are a little shy, you need to attempt to model the behaviour you want your child to pick up on. So, try to be friendly when you meet new people, and confident in social situations (for example, let your child see you asking for directions).

“ My son has always been shy, and I found that what helped was quietly encouraging friendships. I arranged playdates and signed him up for a few out-of-school clubs. I also told him that if people spoke to him and he didn't reply, they might think it was because he didn't like them and that would make them sad. And I told him to ask questions to try and make friends (even if it's just what TV programmes they like). He now tries to speak to others more, and although he's quite quiet, he is happy. ”

Judy, mother of two boys

Shy children definitely benefit from making friends, so playdates and playgroups are great. However, if you think that joining a big group might be too much, take it in small steps. For example, if he starts learning an instrument and gains some confidence, he may be happy to join an orchestra later on.

If you are very concerned about your child's shyness, see him becoming unhappy and withdrawn and think that it is having a huge impact on his life, do speak to his teacher and possibly a doctor or psychologist. The same goes if your child suddenly becomes very shy or quiet when he's always been confident before. There may be a serious underlying reason for this.

BULLYING

Bullying can take place anywhere, at home, online or at school. It's an issue which devastates children and scares parents. The effect of bullying can be horrendous and long term, which is why you need to try to deal with bullying issues as quickly as possible. Physical injuries are usually far easier to deal with (they heal) than emotional. Bullying can sap a child's confidence, leading him to believe he is worthless, and that no one wants to befriend him. So, what can you do about it?

As the Government writes on the Department for Education website, it is "compulsory for schools to enforce measures that will encourage good behaviour and prevent all forms of bullying". If your child has a problem, don't give up. Do your best to resolve it, with the school's help. Every school must have an anti-bullying policy.

What is bullying?

According to the Anti-Bullying Alliance, bullying is behaviour that is repetitious (it happens more than once) and deliberately unpleasant (it is *intended* to hurt another person).

Within this definition, of course, there are many different types of bullying, from calling a child names, hurting him physically or emotionally, or more indirectly, by spreading nasty stories or deliberately leaving him out of a game. Children have a heightened awareness of anyone who's "different" which can mean that a child with special needs or one who wears glasses or has a foreign accent may be at risk of bullying.

Schools are now very sensitive to bullying, although it can be challenging to deal with. Children often fall out with each other, but this does not always mean that a child is being bullied.

It can be difficult (for schools and parents) to distinguish between the kind of teasing which we must all learn to put up with, and nastiness and bullying, which nobody should put up with.

Teasing, in particular, can be a grey area, as friends regularly tease each other. However, if your child is being teased constantly, is not at all happy about this, and has told his "friend" how he feels, then this has crossed the line. Your child will know if there is no humour to the name-calling and if he feels uncomfortable or even intimidated.

Schools have a responsibility to deal with bullying, and you, as a parent, have a responsibility to your child to try to help. This does not mean barging into the school office, claiming that your child is an angel. It does mean sitting down calmly and talking through what's going on. There are (usually) two sides to every story.

Try not to let any negative experiences that you had at school cloud how you view what happens with your own child. Don't be over-sensitive.

> "I was bullied at school and now worry about my children. I just hope that they don't have the same miserable school years as I did. I am sure that a parent whose child is starting school feels apprehensive, but if, like me, you have ever been a victim of bullying, that feeling is quadrupled in intensity."
>
> Andi

What can you do if your child says he is being bullied?

You may have an instinct that something is wrong. Perhaps your child has become increasingly unhappy or withdrawn. He may keep "losing" his lunch-money or come home with cuts or bruises. However, he may not want to talk to you about it.

Children can be unwilling to discuss what's going on, because they feel somehow responsible, and blame themselves. They may also be concerned that any adult involvement could make matters worse.

However, the most important thing is to keep the lines of communication open. You want your child to be able to tell you if there is a problem, and if he won't talk to you about it, suggest that he speaks to another adult that he trusts (maybe an aunt or uncle, or even a teacher). Tell your child not to be ashamed or embarrassed.

If you have strong concerns, you will need to work with the school to address them. Your first port of call should be the class teacher. Explain how you feel and what you think has been happening. Ask if the teacher has noticed any incidents or if your child has seemed unhappy. Don't be confrontational.

Your child's teacher may seem surprised and say that everything seems "fine" in the classroom. Don't be put off by this: a lot of bullying goes on in the playground. Instead, ask if more notice can be taken of what's going on at break-time. More playground staff or older children organising games can make a real difference. You can also suggest that they discuss friendship issues in circle time. See chapter 8 for more on playground issues.

If, after a week or so, you feel that nothing has happened and the bullying is continuing, then speak to the headteacher. Don't confront the parents of any other children who are involved - the school should speak to them for you. I have heard of parents fighting in the playground over bullying disputes (and you wonder where the children pick up the behaviour from).

Discuss the matter frankly with the headteacher and ask for a follow-up meeting a few weeks later. Make sure you have looked at the school's anti-bullying policy and see if it is being followed properly. Make it clear that you will not be fobbed off. Be reasonable, but firm. It helps if you can set up an agreed timeline for the school to report back to you. This may force them into action. You should also put your worries in writing.

Take notes of any conversations you have with the school, and encourage your child to keep a log or diary of what's happening too. That way you have a record.

If you feel that your complaint has not been dealt with properly you can take it to the chair of governors or even the local authority. In more extreme cases, you can raise it with your local MP.

Schools can deal with bullies in a variety of ways, including detentions or even exclusion (although this is rare in primary schools). Many schools now run "restorative justice" systems where bullies and the bullied meet and discuss what has happened. The idea is that the perpetrators can learn about the devastating effects of their actions.

Friends can be a real safeguard against bullies, so encourage your child to make more friends, and invite them over for playdates.

Useful resources

The charity Family Lives, http://familylives.org.uk, has its own social networking site, www.besomeonetotell.org.uk, for parents concerned about bullying.

The Anti-Bullying Alliance, www.anti-bullyingalliance.org.uk, has a wealth of information and resources.

Children can call ChildLine at any time on 0800 1111, or use their website, www.childline.org.uk.

The children's charity Kidscape, www.kidscape.org.uk, can also help.

What if your child is the bully?

It can come as a real shock if your child is accused of actually being the bully. The thought that your child has been hurting someone else, or has been been unkind or malicious, is a message no parent wants to hear. It's awful to find out about this behaviour, either from the school or other parents. You will probably feel extremely ashamed.

However, bullying is a *type* of behaviour and not necessarily a permanent one. You need to find out the facts and then deal with what's going on.

You might even have noticed that your child's behaviour has changed, and may have an idea of why this is so. You could have spotted specific changes, for example in attitude (your child talks about his peers dismissively) or friendships. Some children who have been bullied become bullies when they grow older (even if it's sub-conscious, they want to feel that "power" for themselves).

Being a bully can have long-term consequences for your child, as well as the children he is bullying. Your child will be carrying out a pattern of behaviour which will lose him friends in the long run. It may also mean that he finds it very difficult to develop and maintain good relationships as he grows older. So, your first reaction must NOT be to deny the situation.

How to deal with this

> "We tell parents not to panic. You have to deal with it, and that starts by asking your child to explain their apparent behaviour. You need to explain to your child what is and isn't appropriate. Bullying is not a personality type and that means it can be changed. It might be about re-learning positive behaviour and you will need to reinforce this at home. You will also need very clear boundaries.
>
> Lauren Seager-Smith, from the Anti-Bullying Alliance"

Before you launch into attack mode, you need to ask your child what has been happening at school, particularly with his friends. Although you may be very disappointed, you are still your child's advocate, and need to get both sides of the story.

Do make sure that there is proof of this bullying and that it is not just one child's word against yours. Speak to your child, and if he says nothing has been going on, then speak to the school to find out what they know. Try not to be too defensive, and then work out a plan together.

If you have been given specific examples of your child's behaviour, ask your child if and why he behaved in that way. If you have a younger child, it may be easier to explain the negative consequences and to try and reinforce positive behaviour. Give examples of how friends behave and point out that other people get hurt by the way he is behaving. Some children don't even realise this.

Why are they bullying?

There are a lot of reasons why your child might start bullying others. They range from jealousy to boredom, anger to stress. Bullying gives a child a sense of being in control. Some children bully because they think they will get away with it; others do it because they are insecure or having problems. Bullying dilutes that sense of failure.

Occasional bullying behaviour should not be that difficult to deal with, as long as you stop it as quickly as you can, and understand why it's happening (a new baby in the family perhaps, or arguing between parents). Bullies aren't usually the happiest of children.

Try to work out other ways for your child to relieve his stress (these can even include the old favourite of counting to 10, or judo or karate lessons). If he is suffering because of problems within the family (a bereavement or divorce, for example), you may need to seek counselling for him.

You also need to look honestly at the relationship patterns in your house. Is your house calm? Do your children fight a lot, and physically hurt each other? If a child is being bullied or picked on by an older sibling, he may pick on other children in turn. You may need to change the way you, and other members of the family, act.

If your child has behaved particularly badly, you should try to get him to apologise for his actions. However, do point out that this isn't the end of it. I have heard too many stories of schools suggesting this as the solution, beaming while the bullies apologise to the bullied, and then not noticing when the pattern immediately starts up again. The apology is a starting point only.

A child who bullies may not really be tough. He may be very insecure or attention seeking. You need to let your child know that he is loved, but that his *behaviour* is unacceptable.

SPECIAL NEEDS

Achieving what you want for your child becomes far more complicated when he has special educational needs (SEN). You will need to fight to ensure that he gets the help he needs. SEN is a huge subject, throwing up lots of questions. Here is an overview, and some useful resources for further information.

SEN can cover children who have a problem with communication, hearing or sight, a physical disability or a specific learning difficulty such as dyslexia or dyspraxia (although these are not usually diagnosed until the child is a little older). Although they are put together under the same special needs "umbrella", they are, of course, all very different (and some children may have more than one).

Every school has a special needs educational co-ordinator (usually called the SENCO). She should be involved in each stage of trying to make sure your child gets the education he needs.

Each school also has a special educational needs policy, which sets out how it will help children with special needs, and any facilities it has to do so. Your local authority will also have a specific policy.

When it comes to special needs, parents need to trust their instincts. You need to educate yourself on what can help your child and how you access this. And you have to keep on pushing.

> Don't take no for an answer; never give up. We knew for years before our children were diagnosed that they had significant difficulties. Many professionals we approached were of the opinion that our children were just quirky, that they might well 'grow out of it' or that we should wait and see what happened when they were older, therefore losing valuable time to help them. Early intervention is the key.
>
> Ellen Power, author of *Guerrilla Mum: Surviving the Special Educational Needs Jungle* (Jessica Kingsley, 2010)

When it comes to our educational system, we tend to have a "one size fits all" approach. If your child doesn't fit, then he - and you - are going to have problems. However, extra help is available, if you know how to access it. Schools can offer extra support through teaching assistants, specialist equipment and more. There are also many organisations which can help in your quest to do the best for your child. It can be a tough journey and you will learn a lot. Whatever you do, don't assume that things will automatically fall into place. I have heard of children with hearing problems placed at the back of the class or children with behavioural problems barred from class treats. Ask questions and be aware of what goes on in the classroom. Be sure to make regular appointments with your child's teacher and however angry you feel inside, try to remain polite.

Trust your instincts

If you are worried that your child is falling seriously behind, not behaving like the other children in their class, or being very disruptive, you have to act. Start by speaking to the teacher and then take it from there. She will know if something isn't right.

> "It's a combination of things which might make alarm bells ring. For example, if your child is not at all sociable and has problems with his speech, or if he's not making any progress academically and behaving badly. True, he could be a slow learner, but it could be something more than that. It's hard to get right, but parents need to discuss any problems with the teachers. The most important thing is to get the best for your child."
>
> Claire Blakeney, special needs teacher

Make sure your child always attends any hearing and sight tests, as problems in this area can really affect learning and behaviour. Hearing and vision is usually tested in pre-school or Reception, but this varies across the UK. All children are eligible for free eye tests.

What can you do?

You will know how best to deal with your child, and you need to communicate this to the school. Make sure you meet teachers (including the headteacher and SENCO) and explain anything you feel they really need to know.

Children who have special needs often like routine. They should be placed near the front of the class and asked to contribute to keep them engaged. This is particularly helpful for children with behavioural problems.

If you think there is a more severe problem and your child needs specialist help, you need to push this up a gear. There are different ways in which children with special needs can be helped and they move in a step-by-step approach. Parents can find that their child gets "stuck" at one stage, where they receive some help, but not enough.

During the process, involve as many people as you need to, the class teacher, special needs teacher, headteacher, your GP, health visitor, local authority and specific therapists such as an educational psychologist. Take notes in all the meetings you go to.

Documents you need be aware of

Schools and local authorities follow particular documents when it comes to special needs. Teachers receive guidance through the Special Educational Needs Code of Practice, http://tinyurl.com/654j79u which explains how to assess and then help children with special needs. They use this to decide what kind of help your child needs in school, so it's exceptionally useful if you have a working knowledge of it too.

The SEN Code of Practice can help you access more help for your child. You may find that you need to quote certain sections and show your knowledge of it (for example, if you are trying to persuade the local authority that your child needs to be assessed for a statement).

The special needs register

Some parents have no idea that there are any problems at school until a teacher tells them and suggests that their child is put on the special needs register. This confidential register contains details of all the children who receive assistance.

Schools have to involve you at every stage of helping your child with special needs. When they put a child on the special needs register, it means they have identified that he needs extra help and support.

You should be told of this by your child's teacher or the school's SENCO. You should not simply find out through a letter.

It may make you feel stressed and upset that your child is being labelled, but try not to be. It should mean that they will be getting (at least some of) the help they need.

School Action

The first practical way the school helps is via something called "School Action". This is organised by your child's teacher and the SENCO. It may include one-to-one help for your child from a teaching assistant or enable him to access different equipment, like a laptop so he can type his work.

When your child is put onto School Action, he will be given an individual education plan (IEP). This sets out what problems he has, and also what particular targets the school hopes he will achieve. It also explains *how* these will be achieved and monitored. Your child may have had an IEP while at nursery.

You should make sure you get involved in the discussions, and any reviews, of the IEP (they should be reviewed at least twice a year). Note that IEPs (unlike statements below) are not legally binding.

> "I knew my son had problems at school, but it took a long time before the school agreed to do anything about it. Getting the IEP made me feel that at least something was being done and it has definitely helped. I feel that the younger you get it, the better."
>
> Sadie

School Action Plus

If your child is not making enough progress with School Action, the next stage is School Action Plus. This usually involves professionals such as a speech and language therapist, specialist dyslexia teacher or educational psychologist. The IEPs continue.

It is possible that your child will be put onto School Action Plus straightaway if he has serious problems which the school doesn't feel can be addressed properly through School Action.

Statements

If a school (or very often, a parent) feels that a child needs more help, the next stage is to get the child assessed and apply for a Statement of Special Educational Needs. It may be that your child has a statement before he even starts school, but if not, it can be a long and complicated battle.

Your child does not have to have gone through School Action and School Action Plus in order to be referred for a statement. If it seems that more help is urgently needed, then you can go to the statement stage immediately (although the school may try to persuade you against this, often for financial reasons). Use the SEN Code of Practice to support your case, and make sure you have documentation.

The whole process usually takes around six months. If the local education authority refuses to issue a statement (or even refuses to assess your child in the first place), you can appeal to the Special Educational Needs and Disability Tribunal (www.sendist.gov.uk).

If it's agreed that your child does need a statement, then you will receive a document which will identify your child's needs and then detail exactly how these are going to be met (for example, by a specialist teacher or particular therapy).

The statement is a legal document, so the provision it refers to is a legal requirement. Statements are reviewed each year. You have the right of appeal at every stage.

Most children with special educational needs do NOT have a statement. This may be because their needs are not severe enough to warrant one. However, in some cases, with budgets very tight, it can also be because local authorities do not want to fund them.

Changes on the horizon

The Government intends to alter special needs provision, and announced some tentative plans in March 2011. These included an emphasis on assessing needs at a much earlier stage, when children are in the EYFS, as well as changes to teacher training. The proposals also include scrapping School Action and School Action Plus for a "simpler system" and replacing statements with an "education, health and care plan", whereby education, health and social services work together. This is intended to run from birth to the age of 25. Parents may also be given their own funds to support their child's needs, as well as being allowed to choose which school they want their child to attend – mainstream, special free school or academy. However, all of these are currently in the very early stages and no changes will be implemented until 2012 at the very earliest.

Useful resources

Guerilla Mum: Surviving the Special Educational Needs Jungle, by Ellen Power (Jessica Kingsley, 2010) includes a brilliant explanation of special needs, and how you can help.

ISPEA (the Independent Educational Special Needs Advice, www.ipsea.org.uk) provides free, legally based advice to families who have children with special educational needs.

SOS-SEN, The Free Independent Helpline for Special Educational Needs (www.sossen.org.uk).

Advisory Centre for Education (ACE, www.ace-ed.org.uk).

Family Lives (http://familylives.org.uk).

National Parent Partnership Network (www.parentpartnership.org.uk).

The law on special needs differs in the different countries of the United Kingdom.

For Scotland, see http://tinyurl.com/5t2aak4. There is also an excellent support group in Scotland called Kindred (www.kindred-scotland.org).

Wales also has its own SEN Code of Practice (http://tinyurl.com/5tpohue), and so does Northern Ireland (http://tinyurl.com/6j8bo93).

Being the parent of a child with special needs

You love your child - no one doubts that - and you think your child is special (he is). So, after doing it on your own for the past few years, you may find it hard to let others look after him. However, you do need to let go, at least a little.

It's tough parenting a school child with special needs and you will need to develop a thick skin. Sometimes you may feel alone.

> "For me one of the most difficult things is the patronising way in which some schools deal with you as a parent – almost as if you were also subject to the same special needs as your child. You have to stand up for yourself, as well as your child.
> Valerie, mother of two boys with special needs"

Some parents feel that their child is left out when it comes to playdates or birthday parties. It's perfectly reasonable for you to speak to other parents about this and ask if he can come along - if you promise to accompany him and be responsible for his behaviour. You can also suggest taking other children to events (everyone needs help with lifts). Most parents don't mean to be unfeeling, but some can be thoughtless without realising.

“Charlie frequently fell over, had trouble in the playground, was pushed and pulled, picked last in sports or activities and was generally subtly excluded by his peer group. The parents of his peers were little better – fearing, I think, that his difficulties might ‘rub off’ on their child. It's hard, but you just have to deal with the issues as they arise and do your best to seek advice/input/support.”

Mary, mother of Charlie

Finding an educational psychologist

It can be a real struggle to get even a referral to an educational psychologist. Part of the reason for this may be funding, but it can also be because, with young children, it's not always clear if a problem is an actual special need or a developmental delay which he will grow out of. Many educational psychologists don't assess children until they are 7.

However, educational psychologists can, and will, assess children from the age of 5. If you have real concerns about your child, you may feel that it's worth getting an assessment done at an early stage, although this can be expensive.

“We knew that our oldest son had a problem. He spoke very early and his maths was excellent, but he had major problems reading. Of course, the school said it would come and that lots of children read later. But I knew something wasn't right. The school told us to wait until he was 8, but we couldn't. So we went private. It cost £500 for a three hour assessment. When we were told that he definitely had dyslexia it felt like a real weight had been lifted. Now we knew what the problem was we could do something. ”

Mary, mother of two

You may be able to find an educational psychologist through word of mouth or through the school's SENCO. If not, look through the directory of chartered psychologists (www.bps.org.uk).

Getting a diagnosis

It's usually better to get a proper diagnosis for your child - he will then know why he can't do something, or sees things in a particular way. It also makes it easier to access help.

It can be really traumatic and emotional to feel that your child has been "labelled". But everything I've heard says that a label makes things happen. A diagnosis can also give you the impetus to move forward with your lives and educate yourself about what to do next.

Specific needs

Speech and language problems

You will probably already know if your child has speech, language and communication difficulties and these are the most common special needs for pupils aged 7 or under. According to children's communication charity I CAN, (www.ican.org.uk), a child aged 4–5 should be using well-formed sentences, although there may still be some grammatical errors. He should be easily understood by adults and peers and will frequently ask the meaning of unfamiliar words.

“ If you are worried, talk to people who know your child. Remember, every child is different but go with your gut instinct. If you think that your child needs help, ask a speech and language therapist to see him.

Kate Freeman, qualified speech and language therapist, from I CAN

To find your nearest speech and language therapist, see www.talkingpoint.org.uk/talkinglinks.

Dyslexia

Dyslexia is a specific learning difficulty which mainly affects the development of literacy and language-related skills. It can also affect short-term memory, organisational skills and mathematics. A dyslexic child may have real problems learning to read, write and spell (and often have messy handwriting as well). It can lead to great frustration and under-achievement if it is not addressed properly. Falling behind in basic skills can also affect self-esteem. Dyslexia is not uncommon and around one in 10 of the population is affected.

It can be very hard to tell if a child is dyslexic when they start school, but if you have concerns, it's something which is much better addressed when a child is young.

How do I know if my child is dyslexic?

Dyslexia Action offers a checklist on their website (see below). If the answer to the majority of their questions is "yes", they recommend seeking further advice. Formal identification of dyslexia is normally through an assessment conducted by an educational psychologist or specially qualified teacher.

Try not to get frustrated with your child and his learning. If he is dyslexic, then his brain works differently from yours, and other children's. It doesn't mean he is lazy or stupid.

Helpful resources

Dyslexia Action (www.dyslexiaaction.org.uk)
British Dyslexia Association (www.bdadyslexia.org.uk).

Henry Winkler (The "Fonz" from *Happy Days*) is a dyslexia sufferer and has written a series of children's books, the Hank Zipzer series, featuring a hero who has dyslexia. They are well worth reading.

Barrington Stoke (www.barringtonstoke.co.uk) publish excellent books which will appeal to all children, but are specifically aimed at those suffering from dyslexia.

Autism

Your child may have an autism spectrum disorder (or ASD). It is called a "spectrum disorder" because it can affect each individual differently and symptoms range from Asperger syndrome on one end, to more complex needs (possibly with an additional learning disability) on the other. Autistic spectrum disorders affect more than 580,000 people in the UK.

People with autism have problems with social interaction, verbal and non-verbal communication, and imagination. Role playing can be particularly hard.

They can have real difficulties understanding body language or tone of voice. This can make it very hard for them to empathise or understand what's being meant (as opposed to what's been said), and they often appear to take comments very literally. The world can be a confusing place for people with autism; they often develop particular obsessions and need to stick to a routine to allay their anxiety and be able to get through the day.

If you have a child with autism or Asperger syndrome, then you must communicate with the teacher about how best to help him while at school. You need to tell the teacher how your child's mind works, what motivates him and what his special interests and strengths are. You also need to explain what worries, scares him or makes him happy, and what strategies help to calm him down.

You also need to speak to your child to explain this brand new environment. Emphasise who the important people are (the SENCO, the headteacher), and make sure you are around for any confusing events like school trips. Preparing your child as much as possible for the school environment is essential. Dry runs of the journey to the school and showing photos of the school may also help.

> My son has Asperger syndrome and his education has been a minefield, even though he was diagnosed very young. As a child, he couldn't deal with people dressing up, so when his primary school participated in Red Nose Day he went and hid. I got a call from the head, saying he had locked himself in the toilet and wouldn't come out. 'Unfortunately I'm only adding to the problem, as I'm dressed as Captain Hook,' apologised the head.
>
> Carolyn

As with the other special needs mentioned in this chapter, a diagnosis can be incredibly helpful in prompting action.

It may be that mainstream schools aren't right for your child. In this case, a special school or home-education might be a better option.

Useful resources

The National Autistic Society (www.autism.org.uk) has a wealth of information and provides a number of resources for teachers, such as the Teacher Toolkit. Take a look at this and think of passing it on to your child's teacher.

How to Make School Make Sense – A Parents' Guide to Helping the Child with AS by Clare Lawrence (Jessica Kingsley).

Dyspraxia

Dyspraxia is a neurological problem which affects movement. It can also affect language, perception and thought, and can affect some, or many, areas of a child's development.

Dyspraxic children (and adults) can have problems planning and organising their thoughts, speaking clearly (your child may have had a speech delay) and issues around movement (it used to be known as "clumsy child" syndrome). He may not appear to be right or left-handed, using both hands to do tasks. Unfortunately, dyspraxia is often undiagnosed, which leaves a child to grow up with issues of low self-esteem.

Make sure you speak to your child's teacher if you have any concerns. She may have noticed problems in the classroom, for example with general "clumsiness", or more specifically, with problems using scissors or even getting dressed for PE lessons.

The Dyspraxic Foundation (www.dyspraxiafoundation.org.uk) have a checklist of symptoms on their website. If you think your child meets a number of these, think about investigating further.

Dyspraxia often overlaps with other conditions such as ADHD, Asperger Syndrome or dyslexia.

Hearing issues

If your child has hearing problems you will need to speak to the SENCO and your child's class teacher before he starts school to make sure that the right support is in place. Local authorities also have "teachers of the deaf" who can help to train staff as well as monitor the educational provision for your child and how well it is working.

> "I spoke to the SENCO, Kenzie's teacher and the teacher for the deaf before he started in Reception. I also asked someone from his old nursery to come along to the meeting: she knew more about his classroom behaviour than I did.
>
> The school didn't know anything about deafness or cochlear implants, so I needed to explain things to

them and tell them what Kenzie would need. It's not something people think about it, unless you point out that they need to.

I think the most important thing to get across to the school is that just because a child is able, it doesn't mean he hears everything that's being said. The teacher needs to check that he is following and hearing. You can do this by asking what was said, not just if the child heard (he'll just say yes!). ”

Carly, mother of two boys, aged 7 and 5

If your child wears hearing aids or has a cochlear implant, ask:

- how often hearing aids will be checked and who will do this
- whether the school keeps spare hearing aids and leads in case of breakage
- what training staff will receive on technology for deaf children
- what technology the school will provide (for example, text television or a fire alarm with a visual warning).

Useful resource

The National Deaf Children's Society (www.ndcs.org.uk) produces an excellent booklet on starting school.

BEHAVIOURAL ISSUES

Bad behaviour in school can be a symptom of many things, although it's most commonly tied up with unhappiness and/or boredom. Quite often an unhappy child will play up because he finds school difficult or because he is being picked on or bullied. However, it's also very possible that there are other reasons.

> “Often when a child behaves badly, it has a lot to do with your life and he's reacting to what's going on at home. It might be that your relationship is going badly or that you have money problems, but your worrying can make your child worry too. He may then take it out on other children, see a deterioration in his behaviour or even become a target for bullies himself. Look at how you're doing and think about what effects that may be having.”
>
> Suzie Hayman, from charity Family Lives

When a child is in Reception, he shouldn't really be bored because there is so much to do and so much choice available. If your child is having real behavioural problems, it may be that there is a more serious underlying cause, such as the special needs mentioned above, or perhaps even attention deficit hyperactivity disorder (ADHD). This is the most common behavioural disorder in the UK.

ADHD commonly affects boys more than girls and can be seen in particular by two sets of behavioural problems, inattentiveness and difficulty concentrating, and hyperactivity. A child with ADHD can be very disruptive in a classroom, find it really hard to sit still and be very easily distracted. He will often find it hard to sleep too. A diagnosis of ADHD is usually made between the ages of 3 and 7. As with other special needs, it is helpful to get a diagnosis as early as possible. You can find out more about ADHD and get support from ADDISS, The National Attention Deficit Disorder Information and Support Service (www.addiss.co.uk).

ALLERGIES

All parents feel nervous when their child starts school for the first time, and wonder what they are up to when they're not around to supervise. This becomes even more stressful when your child has an allergy which could be life-threatening. So, is there anything you can do to ensure that your child stays safe at school?

The most important thing you can do is talk to the school before your child starts. This is not a time to be shy. Instead you need to take the lead and set up an action plan – or even more than one – for your child.

You might think that two action plans (these are sometimes called "care" or "health" plans) sound absurd, but you may need one for day-to-day activities (for example, lunchtime) and another in case of emergency. If your child has an epi-pen, inhaler or other medication, then you need to make sure that someone is looking after it and knows how to use it.

Communication with your child is also vital as they need to know what they can and can't touch or eat, and who to speak to in case of any problems.

Many schools take photos of the children with allergies and put them in the classrooms, dining hall and staff room, with details of the issue. Ask if this is a possibility in your school. Make sure that someone takes an epi-pen or inhaler on school trips too.

Food allergies

Awareness is key – yours, the schools and your child's. Speak not only to teachers at school, but also to other parents. For example, explain to them why you would appreciate it if they didn't send snacks containing nuts to school. See pp. 196–197 for more on this.

Make sure the school has piriton or an epi-pen in case of emergencies. And make sure you show the teacher how to use this.

Check when other children have birthdays and pack a special snack for your child on those days, just in case he can't eat the birthday cake that has been sent in to share.

Note: your child does not have to bring in a packed lunch just because he has food allergies. He is still entitled to have school dinners, but discuss any special concerns with the head of catering.

Asthma

Ensure that the school (and that means your child's teacher in particular) knows what may trigger an asthma attack and how to deal with the signs of one. This may be something apparently harmless, like a newly painted classroom.

Your child should be able to take part in school sports without a problem. However, if there is an issue here, make sure your child can flag this up.

Ensure that all your child's medication is labelled clearly with his name and kept up to date.

Useful resources

- www.allergyuk.org
- www.allergyaction.org
- www.allergyinschools.co.uk (has a sample school protocol to download)
- www.anaphylaxis.org.uk
- www.asthma.org.uk

" As a parent of an anaphylactic child, what do I want from other parents? I want parents to understand how hard it is for me to put my trust in them to take care in what they are feeding my child, to trust that they don't just offer out a treat to the kids 'without thinking'. I hope that parents understand me coming on the play date as well as my son, for the first few times, until I have built up a good relationship with the mother for both me and her to

be happy for her to learn how to use an epi pen. I want parents to understand that when my son comes to play I need to go through the menu with them. ”
Viki, mother of two sons aged 5 and 2

HEADLICE

School has many pleasures, for parents and children alike. Headlice is *not* one of these... It is most common in children aged 4 to 11 and it's estimated that it affects around 8% of school-age children.

The lice get transferred from head-to-head contact, so putting a whole lot of children together can be an absolute recipe for disaster, especially when it comes to girls and long hair. I find the whole headlice issue ("nits" are actually the shells of the eggs) rather soul-destroying as you're so dependent on other parents playing their role. One parent's meticulous shampooing, conditioning and combing is utterly useless if other parents aren't checking their children and getting rid of any unfriendly visitors.

Remember you are not immune – if your child has headlice, you will probably soon be scratching away too.

The dreaded critters

Lice cannot jump from one head to another. They can just crawl between or on hairs. They lay their eggs relatively close to the scalp and these hatch in around a week. They only lay a small number of eggs per day (five or so), so if your child has got a lot of lice, they've probably had them for rather a long time.

Lice are not really dangerous, but infestations (and scratching) can lead to interrupted sleep and an unhappy child (and family). If a child gets headlice - or scratches away a lot - other children do pick up on this and can be less willing to be friends.

Word doesn't spread

You may remember the "nit nurses" from your days at school. However, most state schools don't have these any more (many private schools still do). The argument is that they are ineffective, as they can only check which child has lice on a particular day. Experts say that the only way to get rid of lice completely is for the entire community to be treated at the same time, and to continue to check their hair on a regular basis after that. The problem is, parents don't tend to say if their child has headlice, and schools often don't communicate outbreaks to other parents.

Letters announcing that a child has headlice are also frowned upon. In fact, the Health Protection Agency says that "letters notifying other parents of cases have not been found to curtail spread but often provoke itching and anxiety as a psychological response". But if parents don't receive a letter, don't have their children's hair checked and don't know if they have lice, the problem just keeps on going round. And that is a real issue. All too often it doesn't occur to parents to check their children's hair. It might do if a letter/inspection occurred.

> "I am VERY frustrated by the amount of parents who just don't seem to care whether their child has headlice or not. Schools should inform parents when their child starts school that the problem is rife and regular checking is the only way to keep on top of it."
>
> Stevie, mother of two daughters, aged 8 and 4

I feel that when it comes to headlice, educators don't necessarily agree with parents. Many of the parents I have spoken to say they would like to be told if a child does have lice (obviously without identifying them), so they can check their own child's hair and take precautions. But those in "charge" often seem happier for us not to find out. Official advice is not to keep a child off school, even though it might be wise for their hair to be deloused before sending them back. It's worth speaking to your school to see if they do have a headlice policy.

Headlice solutions

There are a few ways of treating headlice. Some parents swear by simple combing and conditioner. Others suggest all manner of other solutions, from mayonnaise and vinegar to olive oil and tea-tree oil.

Be aware that it appears that many humans have built up a resistance to insecticide treatments, and that some of these have a failure rate of 50% to 80%. Non-pesticide treatments do not contain conventional insecticides, which means lice cannot build up a resistance. One of these is Hedrin (www.hedrin.co.uk), which I would recommend.

There are also an increasing number of "repellent sprays" on the market and I use one of these on my daughter. I suppose they are a kind of insurance policy, but I'm happy to use that insurance.

A fine-tooth comb is also essential in the battle against headlice - I'd recommend the nitty gritty comb (www.nittygritty.co.uk). You can also get combs to treat headlice on prescription or from Community Hygiene Concern (www.chc.org) as part of their Bug Buster kit.

One expensive way of eliminating lice is to get others to do it for you! The Hairforce (www.thehairforce.co.uk) is a "headlice spa" which treats children (and, if needs be, their unfortunately infested parents) to a check, vacuum, comb and total destruction of any unwelcome visitors (without chemicals). It's not cheap, but it's thorough and seems to work. At the moment the Hairforce is based in north London, south London and Brighton, but more locations should be on their way.

However you decide to get rid of them, you should comb your child's hair for at least a week afterwards. Parents should also check their children's hair regularly, so please do this for the sake of all of us!

“ Both my daughters and I had headlice unknowingly. I even went to the doctors because I had bites all over my neck and was told it was mosquito bites! I tried and spent a fortune on all sorts of potions from the chemists but meticulous combing was the only thing that really got rid of these blighters! ”

Stevie, mother of two daughters, aged 8 and 4

12

Moving on to the next stage

Your child has finished his first year at school and so have you! Next year there will be new 4-year-olds trooping into Reception classrooms and your little one will no longer be so little. Year 1 heralds the beginning of a different curriculum and the start of more formal learning.

So what issues will your child face as he moves up the school? In this chapter we'll go through some things he might encounter in the years ahead.

TRANSITION TO YEAR 1

Once your child goes into Year 1, the way he learns changes. This is the start of the "National Curriculum".

Unfortunately, some children find the leap between Reception (the Early Years stage) and Year 1 a real struggle. The move from a play-based to more structured curriculum can be confusing and there's much less time for play and being creative (my daughter was unhappy that she could no longer draw and paint whenever she wanted to). Many schools have now cottoned onto this and offer extra help and support. Good schools will make sure that the transition is more gradual. Some incorporate aspects of teaching they used in Reception (keeping some play-based learning, for example) and explain, in advance, what the differences will be.

You can help this transition by:

- encouraging your child to see it as the next stage of growing up
- if you have older children, asking them to explain the differences or to play "schools" showing how different Year 1 can be
- introducing more play or art activities out of school, so your child doesn't think they have all disappeared
- signing your child up for some extra-curricular activities and clubs, which are usually open to children in Year 1 upwards.

Some children are actually much happier when they enter Year 1. These may be the ones who are older for the year, or those who are extremely keen to learn. They really enjoy more formal learning.

THE CURRICULUM

Up until very recently, all state schools followed the National Curriculum. That has now slightly changed, as Academies and Free schools don't have to do so. However, most schools, including private, tend to go along with the National Curriculum in some way (many say they "take the best of it" but enjoy the ability to be more creative and flexible too).

The National Curriculum gives a detailed description of what children should be taught at every level of their schooling, including targets and assessments. Unfortunately for teachers, the details often change (especially with new education secretaries and governments) and this looks likely to happen again soon. Details of the Curriculum are available from Directgov (www.direct.gov.uk) or the QCDA (Qualifications and Curriculum Development Agency, www.qcda.gov.uk).

Many teachers, educationalists and parents complain that the National Curriculum is too narrow and prescriptive and you may be surprised by how little time some subjects (for example, history) receive.

What are key stages?

As you know, children start school in Reception. After this they enter Year 1, and the years continue going up, until they leave secondary school. These years are grouped together in stages.

Key Stage 1 (KS1) includes children in Years 1 and 2 (aged 5 to 7).
Key Stage 2 (KS2) is what we used to call (and some still do) the "juniors". It covers children in Years 3 to 6 (aged 7 until 11).
Key Stages 3 and 4 cover secondary school.

What will they be taught?

Primary schools have a pronounced emphasis on literacy and maths (add science and you've got the "core subjects"). Your child will spend an awful lot of time on these subjects, but they do learn other things too. Compulsory National Curriculum subjects are the same for Key Stages 1 and 2.

They are:

- ICT (Information Communication Technology)
- History
- Geography
- Art and Design
- Music
- Physical Education (PE)
- Religious Education (RE) (although parents have the right to withdraw children from RE lessons if they choose).

Non-core subjects include a modern foreign language, PSHE (personal, social and health education), Citizenship, and Sex Education (which isn't usually taught until KS2).

It's fascinating how, because of the National Curriculum, children in different schools cover the same work. You will soon find that although your child has friends in other schools, they will all be learning about Florence Nightingale or the Great Fire of London at the same time.

In January 2011 the Government announced a major review of the National Curriculum for 5 to 16 year olds. There will now be four compulsory subjects, English, mathematics, science and PE (plus RE, which is still a legal requirement) and Education Secretary Michael Gove said he is hoping to introduce something which is far less prescriptive. Changes to the four main subjects are set to be introduced from September 2013, while the rest of the new curriculum will be phased in the following year. You can find out more about this on the Department for Education website, www.education.gov.uk.

Sats

Schools regularly assess children on an informal basis. They are also formally tested at the end of Key Stage 1 (Year 2) and the end of Key Stage 2 (Year 6). These formal tests are called the National Curriculum Tests, but are more commonly known as Sats (standard assessment tasks or tests). The Government is also soon to introduce a phonics reading test to be taken at the end of Year 1.

The Key Stage 1 Sats are only taken in English and maths, and assessment is done by the teacher. The idea is that they are not seen as "exams" and that children won't know they are taking them. However, some may catch on because they don't usually have to sit quietly doing tests for a few days running!

Your child's results will be given to you on their end-of year-report. Some schools give out more specific information than others (there's more on the "levels" used for marking below).

At the end of Key Stage 2, your child will take more tests in English and maths. These are the biggies (basically mini-exams), and used as the basis for league table results. Because of this, some schools get very stressed and spend much of the final year preparing and "teaching to the test". The tests take place during "Sats week", held in May or June.

There is real concern that these Sats give a narrow focus to the curriculum and mean even less time is spent on other subjects such as art, drama and PE. The current Government is looking into possible changes for KS2 Sats.

Curriculum levels

These can be extremely confusing, so it's worth taking a quick look at this summary. That way at least you'll have some idea of how your child is doing.

The National Curriculum has a series of eight levels which are used to measure your child's progress. You should receive information about what level your child is on both at parents' evenings and in school reports. These levels are also used when it comes to the two more formal tests, at the end of Key Stages 1 and 2.

At the end of Key Stage 1, there are three possible levels which your child can reach.

- Level 1 is the lowest.
- Level 2 is the average level children are expected to reach. It's broken down into:
    - 2(a) (the top of this level; they are nearly into the next)
    - 2(b) (they are securely at this level)
    - 2(c) (they are just into this level).
- Level 3 means they are doing very well, and are at about the standard of a 9-year-old. At Key Stage 1, this level may or may not be broken down for you by the school, so you might be able to find out if your child just achieved it or did so comfortably (or you might not). It depends on the school's policy.
- Level 4 is pretty much impossible for a child to achieve in KS1 Sats because most schools won't let children of this age take the relevant test.

At the end of Key Stage 2, children are expected to achieve a level 4 in each subject, although more able children will reach level 5. However, some children may still be at level 3 (or even below). Once again, levels are also divided into subsections of (a), (b) and (c), with (a) being the highest. In other words, a 5(a) would be the best level you could expect your Year 6 child to achieve.

Many schools continue to use these levels to measure your child's progress as he moves up the school. Children are generally expected to achieve a rise of two sub-levels a year.

> "Sats have always been a hot topic for debate. I was certainly against the testing for a long while, mostly because the children were losing valuable teaching/learning time to endless exam coaching. Taken at face value, Sats should be scrapped. However, I actually feel that children need to be assessed on their knowledge. We can't just keep plying them with information without finding out whether they have understood. It is far more useful and objective to have assessment tools, and have an independent person mark the papers. So instead of scrap the Sats, scrap the league tables!"
>
> Jo Craddock, primary school teacher

There's more detail on assessments on the QCDA website (www.qcda.gov.uk).

Don't get too stressed about Sats levels, especially if you have a child who is young for his year. Some schools provide age-standardised scores, which are more useful. And encourage your child not to worry either. It's true that KS2 Sats take the form of a "proper" exam, which may cause your child to fret, but you should do your best to reassure him that there is no "pass" or "fail".

Note: private schools do not have to enter their pupils for Sats (although some do).

Wales

The Welsh curriculum is similar to that in England, but has recently introduced a more play-based system for the infant years (from 5 until 7). Welsh children learn the Welsh language in school, but do not take Sats. Teachers carry out their own assessments instead.

For more on learning in Wales, visit http://wales.gov.uk/topics/educationandskills/schoolshome.

Scotland

As mentioned in chapter 8, Scotland has recently implemented its new Curriculum for Excellence. There are also no Sats in Scotland.

For more on the Scottish Curriculum visit www.ltscotland.org.uk/understandingthecurriculum.

Northern Ireland

The Northern Irish Curriculum is similar to that in England and Wales, but also doesn't have Sats. As in Wales, teachers carry out their own assessments instead.

For more information about the curriculum, visit http://nicurriculum.org.uk.

MIXING CLASSES

This can be a tender issue, often as much for parents as children! At some point during their seven years at school, your child's class may be mixed with another. This usually takes place either at the end of Reception, or after Year 2 (the beginning of the juniors). However, it can occur at other times and some schools do it every year. Many parents really worry about this, concerned that their children will "lose" friends, or feel disrupted. However, I tend to think that more is made of this than is necessary.

Mixing classes is not uncommon, and occurs for various reasons. These include breaking up cliques, separating difficult children who have ended up in the same class, or mixing abilities. Some teachers claim that children gain better social skills from mixing with a whole new cohort. Friendships can be broadened and children made less dependent on one or two friends. With the younger children, mixing classes is often done if the Reception classes were initially formed according to age. This could mean they are not balanced (in gender or ability, for example) as the children move up the school.

Some schools ask parents to give the names of one or two of their children's friends, so they can attempt to make sure children are put with someone they like when the classes are combined. Be aware that this may add to any stress your child might feel on moving into Year 1. Not only is the curriculum different, but they are with new class members too.

However, my advice on mixing classes would be not to panic! Children are adaptable; I think it's the parents who worry more.

> "The prospect of mixing classes at our school has brought out all sorts of opinions from the parents on perceptions of the 'other class' that they will be mixing with. The Cold War has been recreated in the playground! The kids on the other hand don't give a tuppence and are continuing to have lots of fun at school."
>
> Paul, father of three

I actually think that staying with the same group of children for seven years can be hard. Mixing classes can encourage new friendships and that can't be a bad thing. The only gripe I do have is that the mixing is sometimes done without warning. Schools need to ensure that they keep parents – and children – informed of what they're doing.

> "My daughter's class got mixed 50/50 with the other class when moving from Year 2 to Year 3. It did cause a flutter among the parents; less so among the children. The teacher explained that the classes were mixed a) to balance out abilities in the two classes, b) to separate some children, either from teacher observation or parental request, c) specifically in my daughter's case to separate her from her best friend, because they are of similar ability, and always chose to work together. The teachers felt that they would both learn better separately. There were children who were considered especially sensitive to being split from their friends and they had been kept together."
>
> Deepa

Tips for helping

- Be positive about the change and suggest that this is a way to make new friends.
- Emphasise that your child's "old" friends will still be around in playtimes.
- Arrange early playdates with some of the children who are new to him.
- Speak to the teacher if there are any problems.

HOMEWORK

As your child moves up the school, homework is likely to become much more of an issue. You may soon look back upon the days of Reading Books and learning individual letters with fondness. And if you're anything like me, you may find that homework is taking up far too much of your – and your child's – time.

> "I resent homework. I don't think it really benefits the children; it takes time away from extra-curricular hobbies and uses up family time. I really resent the weekend turning into an extension of the working week. Far too much of it is also done by the parents."
> Rachel, mother of three boys

There are two main issues when it comes to homework – how much there is, and how difficult it can be (for parents as well as children).

Why do we have homework?

The government guidelines for homework suggest an hour a week for Years 1 and 2, one and a half hours a week for Years 3 and 4, and 30 minutes a day for Years 5 and 6.

The idea behind this is that it builds on what children have learnt at school. The aim is to help learning, encourage children to study on their own and also help them to be self-disciplined. It's not supposed to rely on parents teaching their children new concepts.

Homework has long been accepted as something you just have to get on with, and, because it should reinforce what a child learns at school, something that may be boring but is at least beneficial. Schools also try to sell it to you as a chance to become "involved" in your child's learning process. Different schools have different policies on homework and many will mention these in their Home-School Agreement (see pp. 136–137).

Some parents love homework, and actually ask teachers to give their children more. I'm not quite sure why this is so, and tend to be on the other side of this particular fence. In fact, I'm not really a fan of homework in primary schools, except for the essentials. Reading (in the early years), spellings and times tables are okay with me. Projects which turn into competitions to see which parent can build the best model of the Taj Mahal are a waste of time.

For pupils, homework can become far too much of a burden, and doesn't actually seem to enhance learning a great deal (reading for pleasure is as good, and possibly better for their development).

There is no definite link between homework and student achievement. In fact, for primary school children, there appears to be no link at all. A review of 75 years' worth of studies by the University of London's Institute of Education found that the benefits were negligible.

Recently, there has been a backlash against homework, including a campaign led by TV celebrity Kirstie Allsopp. Her children are at private schools, which pile on even more homework. In fact, homework seems to have become a kind of status symbol. Private schools give more than state schools, and assignments often require very hands-on parental involvement.

As a child moves up the school, doing homework can help with exam preparation and possibly time-management skills. But I'm not convinced that children need so much of it.

However, the reality is that most schools do set homework, and that this increases as your child gets older. My advice would be to get your child to do their homework, but not to get too stressed or hung up about it.

> " I find the whole issue of homework difficult. I don't necessarily agree with it at primary school, but don't want to undermine the school and teachers by telling my kids that it's a complete waste of time! So

we do it, but I'm not happy about it. Sometimes I've done most of it myself if I want to get it out of the way.

Sunetra, mother of two ”

Doing the homework

Homework for primary school children often creates a battleground between parents and children. If your child is anything like my daughter, then he or she simply won't want to sit down and fill in homework sheets without much persuasion. You can get round this by threats or bribes ("no computer unless you've done it") which tend to work rather better than the bigger picture ("it's good for you"). As children get older, some schools ask for good excuses why homework *hasn't* been done. This usually encourages a child to sit down and do it!

Some parents I know make their children do their homework on the day they get it, as this then means it's out of the way. Others set aside time at a weekend. You'll need to work out which is best for you, but a regular slot is a good idea.

Remember that homework is meant for your child and not for you. At least let him have a go. After all, it's supposed to increase his knowledge and it also helps him take responsibility for what he does. There is no way that the teacher will be able to gauge how much he has understood if you have completed the work.

Homework is too difficult: for parents

Is your child's homework a struggle – for you? If so, you're not alone. There have been numerous reports and surveys suggesting that although many parents would like to be involved in their child's learning, they don't think they have the right knowledge and skills to do so. Modern teaching methods are often very different, but schools expect us to support our children's learning. This can be a particular problem when it comes to maths and science.

Some schools have caught onto this and now run sessions on understanding the curriculum and how it is taught. I think these are an excellent idea, and would encourage you to suggest it to your school.

Projects

You will either be a project lover or hater. Some parents - and children - relish a longer-term project and the opportunity of getting their teeth into an aspect of Roman or Tudor life, for example, or the history of their house. But they can be very time-consuming, and parents can, all too easily, slip into competitive parenting.

> "The children - and so us - were asked to do a project on their favourite building. I couldn't believe it when my daughter, who's not even 7, said that half the class did power-point presentations! But I was even more dumbstruck when she came home and told me that one girl brought in a model of the Eiffel tower which lit up - the girl's father was an electrician!"
>
> Suzie, mother of one daughter

Helpful resources for homework

Schools can be lazy when they give out homework, suggesting airily that children might like to "look things up on the internet".

However, as you know, the internet is a very big place and you - and your child - might need more direction. You should also not forget the library. Books on particular topics can be extremely helpful. I also found that a children's encylopaedia was a good investment.

The BBC has excellent sites for all ages:
www.bbc.co.uk/schools/bitesize

BBC skillswise is really useful for parents who want to help their children: www.bbc.co.uk/skillswise

The National Archives can help with history homework. Topics are broken down into key stages: www.nationalarchives.gov.uk/education/default.htm

Woodlands School has excellent games to play on their site (also divided into topics and key stages):
www.woodlands-junior.kent.sch.uk/Homework

The Children's University of Manchester has an excellent range of information from Key Stage 2 onwards:
www.childrensuniversity.manchester.ac.uk/

National Geographic kids is great, and very child-friendly, for anything animal or geography related:
http://kids.nationalgeographic.com/kids/

Ask Kids has a very useful and comprehensive School House section:
www.askkids.com

It's also worth googling individual museums - many of them have their own educational resources.

When it comes to maths, I would highly recommend *Maths for Mums and Dads*, written by Rob Eastaway and Mike Askew, published by Square Peg. It explains what your children are doing in school, how they learn maths, and, how you can help. By the time I had finished reading it, I felt as if I could finally assist my children with their homework - rather than confuse them even more by "helping" via my old, twentieth-century, methods.

Your children may use certain sites at school. Ask them – or their teachers – what these are, so you become acquainted with them too. My daughter uses Mathletics, which she can also access from home.

Whatever your views on homework, it's important to show an interest in what your child is up to at school, but there are ways to do this without poring over workbooks. Why not talk to him about his day, and build on what he's done in other ways? You could go to the library together, visit a museum, or discuss what's in the news. Learning an instrument is a particularly good hobby, developing new skills and giving a child an expertise they may then enjoy forever. Children also need free time.

SPELLING

Schools often start spelling tests in Year 1 but they can appear to have a contradictory attitude to this topic. They sometimes don't correct spellings in the children's other work at all – and that can be very confusing for parents.

One of the most common complaints on my blog is that children aren't being taught to spell "properly". One glum father told me that his school called this "phonetic plausibility", while others said that their children's teachers claimed that correcting spelling "stifles creativity". Last year (when my daughter was in Year 3) I asked her teacher why her spelling mistakes weren't being highlighted. She informed me that she "didn't correct spelling mistakes" and added that I needed to "trust her". I was not too thrilled.

All this is not helped, of course, because British spelling is so complicated. Children – even those who are good at literacy – can easily make mistakes and this means teachers are caught in a difficult position. They don't want to destroy a child's confidence by scrawling red marks all over a piece of work, but on the other hand a child does need to be able to spell. Some teachers get round this by adding subtle asterisks where there are mistakes. Others just ignore them! Some schools actually have a "spelling policy", which explains how they teach this topic. It's perfectly reasonable for you to ask to see this.

When it comes to younger children, teachers may only correct the more common words and ignore the rest. They might become stricter on bad spelling as a child moves up the school.

> "You don't fuss too much about spelling until children are writing fluently – at reasonable length, in sentences (this is very different to spoken language), and with a written vocabulary the same as their oral one. But at about Year 3 you've got to start insisting on correct spelling. You also need to encourage children to read, a lot, and by the end of primary school, spelling should be good enough that every mis-spelling can be corrected without drowning the page in red ink."
>
> "Mr teach"

As "Mr teach" says, you can help by encouraging your child to read, and by testing him for any spelling tests, even if he doesn't want you to.

Many children find it far easier to read (working out words) than spell. This is perfectly normal. However, I do disagree with anyone who suggests that spelling isn't important. It is.

Useful resources

Here are two websites which are great for testing spelling:

- www.bbc.co.uk/schools/spellits
- www.timesspellingbee.co.uk

MULTIPLICATION TABLES

It won't be long before your child starts learning his times tables. This may well create an entirely new area for conflict. Learning tables, after all, is not generally seen as fun. And your child may not be learning them in the same way that you did.

Although learning times tables is in the National Curriculum, many schools don't put as much emphasis on them as they used to. This means that your child may not learn them by rote which I think is the best way for most children.

We had quite a battle about this in our house last year. My 8-year-old was learning her tables and wondering why they were important. I told her they were vital, but she remained unconvinced. "Times tables suck!" read a note on the breakfast table one morning.

I, on the other hand, remain convinced that tables really do matter, both for extending maths ability and for life outside the classroom. If you know your tables, then you save time. It also means you won't have problems when it comes to division, and that the maths you come to later, should be easier.

These days there is more emphasis on "fun" and imagination in the classroom. Some teachers dismiss anything which suggests learning "parrot fashion", even though some things (spelling rules, tables) can't really be done any other way. Your school may not encourage learning tables by heart, but I would. You simply *need* to know your tables.

> "By the end of Year 2, children should know their 2x and 10x tables. My own view (which I think is commonly held) is that, once the concepts are formed, the rest should be done by rote, as that's by far the most economical way. It doesn't have to be as boring as in my day, of course!"
> Cathy Beck, primary school teacher

So, what's the best way to learn them?

Every child is different, so what works for one may not work for everyone. Try a few different methods until you find the best one.

> "Start with the easiest table: the tens, which have a simple pattern to them. Follow this with the fives, then the twos and the fours (which are double the twos). The good thing is that many children can grasp these basic tables quickly and will often commit them to memory without needing to formally learn them. When learning tables, it helps to realise that when you multiply, the order doesn't matter, so 3 × 8 is the same as 8 × 3. This almost halves the number of calculations you have to learn.
> Rob Eastaway, co-author of *Maths for Mums and Dads* (Square Peg, 2010)"

There are also lots of electronic ways to learn. "Brain Training" on the Nintendo DS offers quick-fire mathematical problems, while Woodlands School in Kent has some great interactive games online: (www.woodlands-junior.kent.sch.uk/maths/timestable/interactive.htm).

There are also lots of CDs which claim that they will teach your child to remember his tables in a really "fun" way, as they are set to music. I have listened to many of these and can't say that I was overly impressed. However, they might grab your child.

My favourite way of learning tables is via a game, called Perfect Times (www.perfect-times.co.uk). This comes in both computer form and in a card format (which I think is better). Take a look at the website for details of how to play the game.

There are also many patterns within maths and tables. In fact each table has a pattern. The 10x table is the easiest (just put a zero on the end), while the 2x table is just even numbers. There are also other little tricks which may aid memorisation. That bugbear question, what's 7 × 8 can be easily learnt if you remember 5, 6, 7, 8 (ie 7 × 8 = 56).

You can also use the "hands" trick for the 9 × table. Hold your hands out, palms facing you, and fold down a finger to work out the answer. For example, for 4 × 9, put your fourth finger down and you have three fingers on one side and six on the other of the bent finger – hence 36 is the answer. It works for all 9 × tables up to 10.

Learning by rote may not work for all children, and particularly if your child is dyslexic. This is something you need to speak to the teacher about, or to organisations such as Dyslexia Action (see pp. 233–234).

DOES YOUR CHILD NEED A TUTOR?

Peer pressure can be a scary thing – as much for adults as children. You may find yourself feeling perfectly happy with your child's school, and his progress, and then become completely unsettled by the news that "everyone in the class" has got a tutor.

This scary suggestion (about "everyone") is not usually true, although some children may be doing extra work out of school. This does make sense – if the child is struggling with maths, for example, a tutor can explain the problems, calmly and without 29 other children around.

However, if the tutoring is to "get ahead" of the rest of the class, I often think this is more for the parent's sake than the child's. Children need to play and grow up. Teachers will flag up any problems and parents need to stay calm.

School selection and tuition

When it comes to secondary school applications, however, I actually change my views on tuition. And I admit that this is (ironically) partly down to peer pressure! If you want your child to go to a selective school (grammar or private) it is probably sensible to sign him up for some extra lessons, even if it's just to get him used to taking exams.

It's a kind of insurance policy, really, but it's an expensive one (tutors can range from £15 to £50 a session). However, it can be a really good way to build up confidence.

I'd suggest that tutoring doesn't really need to start until Year 5, and even then, once a week should be sufficient. You have to think about your child. Do you really want to hot-house him so much that he gets into the school of your dreams (not necessarily his) but then find it difficult to keep up once he is there?

The best tutors are often booked up a long while in advance, so ring up someone who's been recommended at least six months beforehand and ask to be put on their waiting list.

Tutoring is an unregulated industry, so be very careful. The best way to find a tutor is by word of mouth (although some people jealously guard their child's tutor and won't give out any names!). You could also ask a teacher at your child's school, but they are sometimes a little defensive on this issue (they may think this reflects badly on them). There are lots of tutoring agencies about, and some of them are extremely good. Check that the tutors employed are CRB checked and experienced. Find out if they charge an introductory fee, and if they charge for travel. It's also a good idea to speak to the parents (or child) of someone else they tutored.

Make sure you introduce your child to the tutor to see if they get on. It won't make for a very pleasant situation otherwise. The Good Schools Guide has lists of agencies which it recommends.

“ On deciding to enter my (extremely bright) daughter for the 11+, we ordered a set of past papers and prepared to sit through them together to get a handle on the format. When they arrived, and we found ourselves confronted with a passage from *Tess of the d'Urbevilles* in an English comprehension and a set of Maths questions on topics not touched by her class even at Year 6, it became clear that we would need some extra help, and we were fortunate to hook up with a dynamic tutor. Our daughter thoroughly enjoyed her extra lessons and went on to gain a place with 120 other clever girls at a grammar school. She is having a wonderful time, working at her own level at last. Realistically, I believe she would have had far less chance of getting into the grammar school without the tuition, but that doesn't make me feel happy about it. ”

Matt

FRIENDSHIPS

We discussed friendships in chapter 6, but as children grow older, friendships do tend to become more complicated. This can be painful for parents, as they watch their children (especially their daughters) fall in and out of being "best friends".

“ As children get bigger I think the friendship thing does become really important. It really matters for a child to have a group, or even one or two people they can turn to for help to get through the sometimes long day. The playground is a microcosm of the real world, with bullies, leaders, followers, negotiators and jokers, and it is up to our children to work out where they fit best and find the friends that are best for them. It's all part of

letting go and watching them grow as their own people.
Juliette, mother of three children aged 10, 7 and 4 ”

Remember that school isn't everything. Out-of-school clubs and organisations such as Cubs or Brownies can be excellent ways for your child to meet other children. This is a problem with after-school clubs held on school premises - it means your child is mixing with the same children again.

Girls' friendships are often more intense than boys. This is partly because girls love to talk, rather than play football, and can become very close. However, talking can then become bitchy, especially when it's about other girls in the class. Girls can also become extremely upset when friendships change. Group dynamics shift all the time.

One of the most crucial things you can do is keep on talking to your child. Keep those lines of communication going, so that if there are any problems, your child feels that she can talk to you. Then you can be a sympathetic ear, but also give her another perspective on what's going on.

Boys' friendships are often easier. But of course, not all boys want to play football and it can be hard on those who don't.

“ I think boys are far simpler in all things and friendship for boys is a much more honest matter. When boys fall out they have a fight (physical or verbal) and that's it – no holding grudges, going behind backs, dirty looks, etc. To me boys are like puppies – love, food and exercise appear to be the recipe for a happy boy.
Lisa, mother of a daughter, aged 11 and son aged 7 ”

If your child is having real problems with friendships at school, talk to the teacher as she may be able to help.

BIRTHDAY PARTIES

We covered this topic in chapter 6 too, but it's sure to rear its head again as your child moves up the school.

What often happens is that boys and girls move into a world of separate parties, rather stereotypically along gender lines (lots of football parties for the boys and princess/pyjama parties for the girls).

> " By Year 1 or 2, the parties change. My son's friendly with lots of girls, but when their mums come up to me and say "sorry, it's just girls", I don't worry about it. It just follows the natural pattern of the kids. "
>
> Katrina

Parties often become much smaller (perhaps six or eight children) as a child gets older. For example, they may go to a bowling alley or cinema.

If you have a child who is friendly with girls and boys (not actually that uncommon), ask them what they want to do. They may want a small mixed group to celebrate with, or they may go for a gender-specific party after all. Never invite *nearly* all the girls or boys, missing out just one or two, as that is really hurtful.

If you are friendly with a parent, and your child is no longer friendly with their child, don't force your child to invite them to his party. If you feel the need, you could explain this to the parent in question (carefully, of course!).

SPORT AT SCHOOL

The amount of sport at school really depends on what kind of school your child attends, although most private schools have better sporting facilities than state. In my opinion, there is not enough sport played at my children's school – and no element of sporting competition at all.

One major problem is that many schools don't have sporting facilities and playing fields have been sold off. Many teachers no longer want to spend their free time coaching sport and, unfortunately, sporty children tend to play their sports at clubs outside school hours. However, it is important to encourage your child to take part in sport at an early age.

> "My daughter is deaf and struggles with academic life at school. Her whole life so far has resulted in her being labelled 'average' as she plods on through all her different subject 'tests'. As a gangly 12 year old she has recently found she can run long distance, and win! You just have to look at her face to see the excitement and joy. Why did she have to wait until secondary school to feel like that when others had that feeling through school tests from age six? If there is competition in academic tests there should be competition on the sports field."
>
> Eddie

PE is part of the National Curriculum, but it's not a big part. In Key Stage 1, children will take part in some combination of dance, games and gymnastics twice a week, but dancing to nursery rhymes never really appealed to my daughter! In Key Stage 2, they continue with these, but add in athletics, "outdoor pursuits" or swimming (still only for two sessions a week). If your child doesn't take part in swimming in Key Stage 1, then he will have to do so in KS2.

The Government has promised to put an element of competitive sport back into their revised curriculum.

Swimming

At some point, your child will have to do swimming at school. Some love it; others don't enjoy it at all.

> "My son's school does swimming in Year 2 and he is already worrying about it (he's only in Year 1). He absolutely hates having water on his face and I just don't know how he will cope. It's such a struggle even washing his hair!"
>
> Dina

The problem with school swimming is that it takes so long. Few schools have swimming pools on site, so children have to be transported, by foot, bus or coach, to the nearest one. Some of these pools have unpleasant changing rooms (which children can hate), while other children simply don't like hanging around, shivering by the edge of the pool. Even those who enjoy it often complain about how little time they actually spend in the water. One Ofsted report found that the time it took to get a class to the nearest pool was sometimes twice as long as the lesson itself.

You may also be asked for a "voluntary contribution" towards any transportation, or be asked to come along and help. However, be warned that this can take rather longer than you expect, and involves lots of hanging around.

Learning to swim is a compulsory part of the National Curriculum and government guidelines state that by the time children complete primary school, they should be able to swim 25 metres. Many children don't actually reach this level, and if you're determined that yours should, sign up for out-of-school lessons.

MOVING TO A PRIVATE SCHOOL

Some parents choose to move their child to a private prep school aged 7, after the end of Key Stage 1 (Year 2). This may be for a variety of reasons, but commonly includes a greater emphasis on academia, better facilities (especially for sport) and smaller class sizes. If you're considering this, don't forget to ask your child his views: if he is happy and thriving at school, you need to ask yourself if you really need to move him.

Children who want to start at a private school will have to take an exam or be assessed, and depending on how well they do, they will then be offered an interview. This will usually involve some reading and comprehension as well as some pretty gentle personal questions (what he likes doing or what television programmes he enjoys). It's also not uncommon for a child to be asked to tell a joke (why? I'm not sure. Perhaps to show that he is well rounded!), and your child should probably have a (clean) joke prepared.

Most private schools will also ask to meet you, the parents. Always be polite, friendly and interesting in these interviews.

The jump from state school Year 2 to a private prep school can be hard. The best prep schools want children who are already doing extremely well in their studies, and your child will probably be up against those from pre-preps who will have been well drilled for exams. You may want to hire a tutor (see pp. 263–264) to ensure that your child is on a level playing field.

Private secondary schools

When it comes to private secondary schools, your child will definitely have to take an exam and a tutor's good for this, even if it's just to acquaint your child with exam procedure.

Once again, your 10- or 11-year-old (and you) will be interviewed, possibly by the head or deputy head, or perhaps by subject teachers. Children are sometimes interviewed in a group, partly to see how they interact with their peers.

The best tip I can give you is not to over-rehearse your child. That risks him coming across as rather boring and colourless. Schools want to take on children who they will enjoy teaching. However, do ensure that he is smartly dressed and encourage him not to fidget or bite his nails!

THE NEXT STEP: SECONDARY SCHOOLS

Finding out about and applying for primary school was hard. Sadly it's no easier when it comes to secondary schools. It's absolutely vital for you to start thinking about secondary schools *before* your child enters Year 6. There may be all sorts of application criteria which you need to address a year or so ahead (for faith schools, for example), and if you're choosing a school which selects its pupils in some way (either academically or in a particular area such as music), you may want to think about hiring a tutor. You should plan to go on Open Days when your child is in Year 5.

Don't choose a school on the basis of your child's friendships (or yours – the "school gate" scenario is completely different at secondary school). He will make new friends, and you need to make sure he goes to the right school for *his* personality and abilities. When you visit a school, always remember that there is one great question you can throw at a teacher: would they send their own child there?

" Getting a child into secondary school is the single biggest educational challenge facing most parents of children aged 8–11. Our school system is incredibly confusing. The choice is wide – state or independent, mixed or single sex, local or in another borough, grammar, crammer, faith, boarding, special needs. . . Parents are required to visit, fill in a multitude of confusing forms, navigate the catchment areas dilemma, supervise practice papers with their child, and stay sane. Parents feel overwhelmed by the process.

Katie Krais, from Jaderberg Krais Educational Consultancy ”

Start early

Find out about local schools in Year 4 or 5. Make sure you do your own homework and don't simply listen to others – you'll soon find that there are lots of opinions out there. Remember what you did for primary schools and once again look up Ofsted reports, find out about schools near you, and speak to parents who live nearby.

Acquaint yourself with the admissions criteria of any of the schools which interest you. Check if they have a banding system. Banding simply means that a school admits pupils with a range of abilities. It also means your child might have to take an exam, in order to be put into the right band.

Take advantage of parents' evenings at school to find out how your child is doing. Many teachers don't give very specific information, so you may need to press them. There is no point entering your child for a selective school if they are not going to get in, or manage the work once they are there.

“ I'd definitely recommend visiting and speaking to pupils if you can. You can get such a feel for a school if the person showing you around is polite, helpful and enthusiastic. It's true for the children too. Mine definitely 'took' to the school during an open evening. It's a question of whether they can 'see' themselves there in a year or two.

Annie, mother of three ”

You also need to think about distances and the school run. Many children make their own way to secondary school. Find out what public transport is like or if there is a school bus.

And don't forget your child's own opinion. You need to ask him what matters. If he is very sporty, then you need to look for a school which emphasises this. If he is shy, then perhaps a huge school may not be the right place for him. Wherever you choose, you want him to be happy.

Hopefully you and your children now have all the information you need to survive starting school. I can't promise that the next seven years won't ever be stressful or frustrating, but they should also be enjoyable. And ultimately, I hope that, like me and my children, you find them rewarding. Good luck!

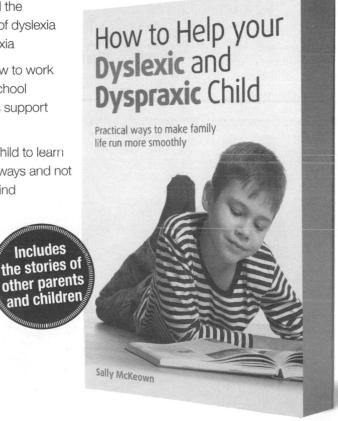

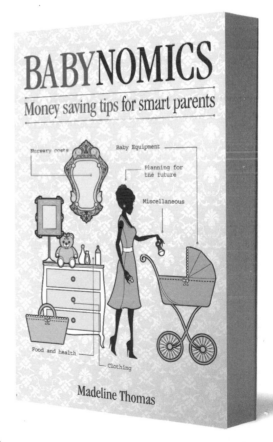